Introduction

The Pulps! What can we say that other creators haven't said before?—with probably better words. If you're reading this, then you already know all about those adrenaline shots of pure entertainment–their hardboiled covers with artwork that *bitch-slaps* your attention span into paying attention–and all the greats that came out of that world: Philip K. Dick, Robert E. Howard, Robert Bloch, H.P. Lovecraft, Donald E. Westlake, and too many others to name here without boring you to tears.

But if you slipped on a banana peel and stumbled your way into finding our *Instagram* page or this book in magazine format and don't know what in tarnation Pulp Fiction is, let us enlighten you about our *Pulpy religion*. And no, Pulp Fiction are not stories about people drinking freshly squeezed orange juice. It's not just the name of Tarantino's masterpiece second film or only the art found in the thrilling cheap magazines that were famous in the first fifty years of the 1900s. Pulp Fiction is a style. A state of mind. A way of life. If you value entertainment more than any type of "teachings," "awareness," or "the message," then you my friend, are a *Pulp Believer*.

If you're rolling your eyes by now, thinking, "Yeah, yeah, get on with it. I gotta go watch whatever *'content'* Netflix is shoving down my throat. And I've seen these types of new pulp anthologies before and was not impressed," then by all means go. Thank you for making it this far, though.

But if you stay, you will find bite-size creations that touch upon the Pulps' most popular genres: Action, Horror, Romance, Mystery, and Sci-fi. *We have Pirates, Slashers, and Weirdos, Oh My!*

These five stories explore synchronicities, fears of car crashes, phobias of big cities, and the questioning of our roles in modern societies.

But what we really offer that's different from all the others that came before us is that we go against this "*Me Me Me*" trend that's been destroying what Independently produced Art is all about. Indie Creators have been brainwashed into believing that they must step on each other to find success. The "*oh-yeah-that's-good-but I won't say it or support it because it-will-take attention-away-from what I'm-doing*" chip has been firmly implanted into the back of their brains. They don't realize that the only competition we *Indies* face comes from Major Corporations. It's basically the same attitude that's been killing Rock and Roll. Unsupportive attitudes, too much infighting, too many gatekeepers–Rockabillies looking down on the Metalheads, Metalheads criticizing Punks, Punks hating Goths, Goths making fun of Emos–none of them ever realizing that if the music invokes a Rock and Roll spirit (guitars, bass, drums) then all of them are part of the same family. If you give our work a chance, shrug and say, "Bah, I can do better than that," then tell us! Without being a jerk about it. We will find your work, support it, enjoy it, review it, and admire the hell out of you for creating it. That's what *Neo-Pulps!* is all about.

We want to thank all the entertainers and creators who helped make us this way:

Joe Bob Briggs and Darcy the mail girl from The Last Drive-in, for creating a supportive Mutant family where everyone is welcome and all horror creations are appreciated. Creature Features' Vincent, Tangella, and Livingston, for bringing back the classics and giving us thousands of hours of

4

Pulpy entertainment. And finally, independent filmmakers Wigwolf and B. Harrison Smith for setting up inspiring examples that we all should follow: To hell with the critics, just make your art!

A warning about this Issue: At *Neo-Pulps!* we hold freedom of speech and artistic expression in the highest regard. We respect everyone's beliefs and opinions and never aim to offend. Our fictional stories are just that. FICTION. They're NOT personal opinions or views of anything. We just want to entertain our audience. So, if you are easily offended by what FICTIONAL characters do or say in FICTIONAL stories, please stop reading right now and never pick anything published by *Neo-Pulps!* again, thanks for stopping by.

It's a Pirate's Death for Me

December 1564

A gray mist covered the morning sky. It drifted through the beach like the ashes of a funeral pyre, blocking the horizon from all eyes. The feeling of being caged forced Captain Warren Reis to take a deep breath of the cold, salted air as his black Cavalier boots landed on shore. His first mate, Benson, was preoccupied with preventing their small, jolly boat from drifting away with the incoming tide.

"It's fine where it is." Reis's square bearded jaw gestured towards the many other barnacle-encrusted jolly

boats scattered around the border of the shore. "We may be the last ones to arrive. Let's make haste."

They hurried through the mist, following the footprints in the sand that led them into the jungle surrounding the cathedral where the meeting would occur. Only their footsteps and the waves behind them could be heard as they navigated through the foreboding shapes of many decaying trees.

Reis's instinct took the lack of critter-clatter as a bad sign. His calloused hand rested on the handle of the cutlass hanging from his belt, the blade ready to swing out from its sheath and strike down any threats.

Above the trees, the corroded dome-top structure of the cathedral came into view, and they began to hear voices in the distance. Their alertness eased when they arrived at a clearing in front of the cathedral and were greeted by a small crowd of rough, familiar faces.

These were around forty of the most notorious pirates of the seven seas, gathered in separate clusters and all sharing a miasma of anxious anticipation.

Reis stood there. His tall, powerfully built, and darkly dressed body drew the attention of all the eyes before him.

Even though some had to squint, they all recognized the black leather tricorn hat—with the silver raven pin on the right side—and the long dark hair, beginning to show grey strands, flowing from it. But it was the burn scar across Reis's bronzed forehead that unmistakably let all know he was the Captain of The Raven crew.

Reis had gained infamy not by accumulating the most gold or having the biggest armada but by being the only pirate mad enough to fight the Royal Navy head-on and win by setting all their ships on fire, causing an inferno on the royal port. This feat earned him the nickname Reis the Blaze. Benson's small, slender figure paused at his side like an extra blade waiting to be commanded.

"By gods!" Captain Quetzal bellowed from the crowd of marauders, cutting through the momentary silence. He approached Reis, followed by his first mate Doc Testudin and another crewman Reis failed to recognize.

"We was wondering if them things didn't—" Quetzal words fell faster than a bottle after all the rum had been drunk. The forced smile dominating his round, red face disappeared. He swallowed hard before changing the subject. "Glad ye made it, old blood. Too many Youngens here. Things are *disbalanced*." Quetzal, captain of the Aztec crew, was one of the oldest living pirates that Reis knew. He still had a head full of long, bushy white hair that escaped from a dirty calico head scarf and seemed to be connected to his equally white beard. Being overweight, with a face constantly covered in sweat–even in cold temperatures–and overall looking like he could drop dead at any moment didn't stop him from ruthlessly destroying any adversary who dared cross him.

He pulled a big silver flask from his hip pocket and took a long pull, the many lines on his face scrunched in the process, like a wrinkled map. "*Ahhg*, that'll put hair in ye mum's back," he belched and offered Reis the flask. Reis declined, knowing Quetzal's liver was only satisfied by pure alcohol mixed with sugar.

"What the captain is trying to say is that we are happy you did not perish at the hands of those infernal things attacking our way of life. If indeed they do have hands." Doc adjusted the bridge of his Tortoiseshell-rimmed glasses with one finger. He kept his long blonde hair secured in a ponytail, and his clean-shaved, aristocratic face didn't reveal the merciless acts of piracy that had gained him the honor of being Captain Quetzal's right-hand man.

"There ye go again trying to put them fancy words in me mouth," Quetzal complained. "And what did I say 'bout giving attention to them things?"

"The whole point of this meeting, Captain, is to bring attention to those things," Doc reasoned, looking at Reis and Benson for validation. But Reis was scanning the profiles of the other pirates, seeking hidden expressions of treachery–he found none–and Benson's face was partially covered by a long brown hat. The only visible smooth features revealed nothing.

While Quetzal and Doc continued to argue, a couple of older pirates came to greet Reis. Soon, a small group had formed around them. Bottles of rum were passed around, along with stories of the old days. All of them avoided mentioning the horrible things that had brought them here.

"Aye, those were the days," Quetzal was saying with a surprisingly sober tongue. "Smooth sailings, pure open seas. And only if a boyo dared spit in yer eye or the blasted royal navy came sniffing up yer bum did ye have to raise pistol and sword. Otherwise, the smooth sailing and the flowing rum would continue." His bloodshot eyes turned towards a small group of tattooed, scrawny Youngens laughing and posturing in front of the closed doors of the cathedral. "Now, these Youngens are all under the illusion that a pirate's treasure is painted in silver and gold. They're ignorant of the fact that freedom is a pirate's true treasure. And that a good day's plundering is a hefty sum of food and drinkable water."

A circle of nods and grunts of agreement followed his words.

"You forgot the rum and the leaf, gramps," a raspy voice said from an approaching group. "Without 'em a good day's plundering is incomplete." The voice belonged to Captain Lizard Morrison of the Wassailer crew. He cackled and teetered his way into the circle of reminiscing pirates.

"Surprised to see you here, Morrison," Reis huffed. "Must be a sign of how desperate we have become." He considered the Wassailer crew to be just one step above the anarchistic Youngens. Morrison never formed alliances with other pirates or lent them a hand when in need. And he carried the bad reputation of starting fights just for laughs. His only admirable quality was his hatred of the royals and all manner of authority.

"*Iss Captain* Morrison to you, *Blaze*," Morrison smirked.

"Heed your own words." Reis glared down at him.

Morrison cackled loudly without reason. "Good ol' Captain Blaze." He shook the curls of his long brown hair, exposing the many golden earrings scaling the shells of his ears. "Ever feel like setting your own ship on fire?"

"Best watch yer mouth, boyo." Quetzal offered Morrison a bottle by shoving it into his exposed chest, making him sway a little. "We here in a camerade-way. Don't ye go looking for brawls just outta boredom."

Morrison smiled and shrugged, accepting the bottle being offered. The cold didn't seem to bother him, although his shriveled-up nipples said otherwise. His mocking tone urged a buffet of Reis's brawny fists, but they weren't here to fall into childish squabbles, so his fists remained still.

As Morrison drank, Reis peered past him towards the cathedral. The building loomed over them, casting an aura that was as old as the legends of Tartaria.

Suddenly, its big ancient double doors began to open. Silence struck the pirates again.

A few steady hands rested on the handles of weapons while the most nervous ones just went ahead and drew pistols and swords. The tension remained even when they all saw that Captain Ormond–the man who had called the meeting and the only man they all trusted enough to make them show up–was standing at the entrance. Ormond surveyed their faces with his left eye. A red eyepatch covered his right one. His trimmed hair and mustache were the color of rusty steel. He wasn't as tall or muscular as Reis but still commanded as much respect.

"Gentlemen. Let us begin," he simply said before returning to the shadows of the cathedral.

"Who's he calling *gentlemen*?" Morrison asked no one in particular, stumbling forward. "It's an insult to my scallywag nature."

The pirates plodded their way into the cathedral, with most of the Youngens leading the way. Reis and Benson took their time, letting all the others go in before them. Grime covered the iron-barred windows, and only the light of candles hanging from the walls illuminated the large empty space inside of the cathedral, leaving shadows lurking in every corner. A stench of mold, smoke, and dust replaced the fresh, salty air.

I was right. Tartarian masonry, Reis thought, studying the columns and the many cracks on the long stone walls. He was the last one to enter, and the doors were immediately closed behind his back, prompting him to pull out his cutlass. "What's this? Why are you trapping us here, Ormond?" Reis shouted.

Benson backed him up with a pistol in hand. The other pirates shared his protest, drawing their weapons.

Through the shadows covering the doors, Reis saw the two figures who had closed them. They were camouflaged by hooded dark robes which hid any distinguishable features.

"Who else is here with you? Better answer fast, or I'll slash my way out!" Reis didn't remove his gaze from the hooded figures.

"Spit out an explanation!" Quetzal yelled at Ormond.

Ormond–waiting behind a broken-down altar at the far end of the cathedral with four hooded figures standing behind him—spread his hands. "Comrades, please, settle down. It's for our own protection. What we need to discuss—"

"We can discuss with open doors!" Reis interrupted.

Shouts of agreement followed his words.

"You all have trusted me enough to come this far," Ormond pleaded. "Just listen to what I have to say."

Spitting and cursing, the pirates complied, not letting their guards down. Ormond had earned their trust by being one of the few medical men who used his skills to mend the wounds of all marauders, for a small price of course. But his skills went beyond the medical field. He also started a network of safe passages for pirates. It didn't matter if they had bounties high enough that even their own mothers would sell them out. Reis and his crew used Ormond's skills many times. The scar on his forehead was a testament to that fact. So keeping an eye on the hooded figures, he waited and listened.

"You all know that we are being hunted," Ormond began, struggling with his words. "But not by the Royal Navy as on most days. This new enemy comes for us at night, not to apprehend us but to massacre our crews!"

"What are they?" Morrison shouted from a corner. A rare, somber look appeared on his face. "Quit stalling. Tell us what you know already."

Ormond dropped his one-eyed gaze, his hands squeezing themselves by his sides. "I don't know what they are. But I know what we can do to protect ourselves and our way of life." A hooded figure handed him a black leather-bound book. He flipped through the pages, keeping his head down, shoulders slumped forward. His posture and the tone of his voice told Reis what he needed to know.

Reis cursed himself for letting fear guide him here. *Or had it been pride?* One involuntarily glance toward Benson reminded him it had been neither. When word came down that pirate ships were being found un-plundered, with decks covered in blood and half-eaten or disemboweled crewmen, he knew there was something wrong with the nature of this new enemy. But instead of fleeing, as some of the pirates who lacked a spine had done, he came here looking for a way to fight back and protect their way of life.

The old ways. Our desperate clinging to it has blinded us to put too much trust in one man, Reis thought. *And here he has us now,* he glared at Ormond. *Trapped in a forgotten cathedral left behind on this small, phyton-shaped isolated island. What bloody fools we have become.* His gaze returned to the hooded figures and the doors behind them.

"The British empire is preparing to go to war with the King of Spain," Ormond continued. "And they're in desperate need of manpower. Especially, of the ruthless kind."

"And how does that concern us?" Doc asked.

"Her *majes*–the Queen, has sent these men," he gestured at the hooded figures, "to offer us a deal. In return for our eternal faithful service, not only will the empire pardon us, but they will protect us from what has been attacking our comrades at night."

The inside of the cathedral exploded with shouts of protest and all manner of foul curses.

"Tell that bloody Queen she can go piss on her mum's grave," Quetzal yelled, throwing a bottle past Ormond's head. It missed the hooded figure behind him.

"*Ma* fellow freebooters! Listen up!" Morrison bellowed. His usual smirk had returned. "I wasn't really paying attention.

But I think what Ormond's trying to say is that he brought us all

the way out here, all *secret-like*, just so we would bow down and kiss the Queen's royal bony *bunda*!"

"*Aye!*" the pirates around him agreed.

"I thought so. We're done here," Morrison told his crew. "I'm bored outta my mind. Let's get those doors open." They started moving towards the exit, and others followed.

"And how are you going to protect yourselves tonight? Or tomorrow night!" Ormond shouted back. His words stopped some of the men in their tracks and made others hesitate. "The Crown is not only offering us protection, but it will also let us keep all the spoils of any enemy ships we raid."

In the front row, the eyes of a skinny Youngen lit up. "*Spoils!*"

"Spanish gold!" His crewmates shared his salivation.

While in the back row, Reis became more disgusted. The scar on his forehead burned with rage. "You best step out of my way," he told the hooded figures.

They didn't budge.

"And ye vouch for this deal?" A blonde Youngen asked Ormond.

"Aye. I give you all my word. It's a solid deal." Ormond showed the open book. Hundreds of red ink signatures filled its flesh-like pages. "Once you sign this book, you will be known as a Privateer working under the protection of the British Empire. You can sail, drink, and plunder freely without having to constantly look behind your back."

"*Privateers!*" Quetzal cleared his throat for a nauseatingly long time, reaching deep into his mucus reserves, and then assaulted the floor by spitting out a yellowish-green wad. "*Tha'* what I think of ya' offer. Ye can call a turd *rose,* and it'll still smell shitty. Sign that eldritch book, boyo, and a slave it's all ye ever be."

"A slave filthy with gold!" The skinny Youngen grinned, and his remark elicited cheers and whoops of approval from his mates. "I'll sign. Have you ink and pen?" he asked Ormond, stepping forward.

"Your name," Ormond raised his head to face the Youngen, "must be signed with your blood."

And it all became clear in Reis's mind. *Eternal faithful service*. He studied the hooded figures more closely without letting his body betray a shudder. They hadn't moved an inch since Ormond started his speech. Not even to take a breath.

"Prepare yourself," he whispered to Benson, then pulled out his pistol and fired at the hooded figure on the right. The bullet penetrated its chest, but no blood spilled out.

The crowd turned their heads towards the doors.

"*Did ya see*, Cap'n?" One of the Wassailers asked Morrison, terror twisting his hardened features. "Didn't even flinch! 'Tis the devil's work?"

"Don't know. But I'm no longer bored." Morrison unsheathed his straight, double-edged sword.

"Don't attack them!" Ormond warned. "They won't harm you if you don't fight them."

"Then get them out of our way!" Reis yelled back.

Benson fired at the other hooded figure and was met with the same result.

The Wassailers, the Aztecs, and other pirates merged, forming a group with Reis and Benson in the lead.

"Matter not if they be devils," an Aztec crewman roared, lifting his spiked iron mace. "If the Captain says move, they best jump outta the way." He swung the mace towards the head of the hooded figure on the right. The hooded figure's clawed left hand grabbed the mace while its right shot out with the darting quickness of a tentacle. Its claw slashed the crewman's throat. Blood dripped down his neck, soaking his neckerchief. Then, with a gurgling sob, he sank down, and his face kissed his own blood as it stained the floor.

"Ye hellish scum!" Quetzal fired at the hooded figure, igniting a storm of bullets from the pirates on his sides that did nothing but put holes in the black robes of the figures.

The sight of the crewman's blood awoke the hooded figure on the left. Its claws found a couple of pirates, and a few seconds was all it took for the floor to be littered with their flesh, blood, and crimson-soaked shredded clothes. The other figure released the mace, preferring to use its claws to attack. In a frenzy, it managed to slaughter the life out of six crewmen before Quetzal, Doc, and Morrison held it back with their swords.

When the pirates started firing, Reis and Benson stepped back to reload their own Flintlock pistols. Now that almost all those men lay dead on the floor, the hooded figure set its sights on Reis. It leaped toward him and was met in midair by his sharp cutlass. The blade slashed the figure cleanly through the torso. Its legs dropped on the floor with its upper body falling on top of them. The wounds emitted a foul, fishy smell. The stench of a watery death.

Rushing around it, Benson tried to get the doors open but couldn't find a latch or lock.

Reis kicked the doors. "These are shield-doors, built to keep the enemy from entering. They have no keyholes, but an opening lever must be somewhere at the end of this room." He looked toward the altar and spotted a short silver rod protruding from the middle of the left wall. His eyes briefly noted the conflicted emotions that ran through the pirates in the middle of the crowd. Some kept looking back and forth between the bloody fight in front of the doors and Ormond behind the altar, convincing the Youngens to cut the tip of their fingers and sign the book with their blood.

"Won't this thing die!" Doc gasped. They had stabbed the hooded figure multiple times and cut one of its arms, but it came striking at them with the other. Until, with a dashing blow, Morrison chopped off its hooded head.

"Sorcery!" Quetzal exhaled, looking down at the figure that Reis cut in half. The upper half of it was drinking the pool of blood on the floor like a dog lapping up spilled wine.

Reis stood motionless for a few seconds. The horror that sometimes infects the demonically possessed crawled through his skin. "We found an answer here, after all." His voice sounded strange even to himself. "These are the things that have been attacking our mates."

"And he wants us to work for them?" Doc's face paled.

"Not for them! With them!" Ormond was holding the book while the Youngens signed. A line formed behind them; pirates both young and old were ready to sign. "The Queen can only use them in the darkness. And now she needs our services during daylight."

"After she sent them to feed on us!" Reis pushed the point of his cutlass through the creature's hooded skull as it continued to drink the blood of his mates.

"They are us!" Ormond grated, glassy-eyed. "These hooded men were part of my crew. All of you knew them when they were alive just a few months ago before we were attacked."

"There you have it, fools." Reis yanked out his cutlass from the creature's skull. It had finally stopped moving. "This is what eternal faithful service means. Even after death, you'll be the Queen's loyal undead sea dogs!"

Seconds of heavy silence hung in the air, along with the stench of death and gore.

"You won't end up like them if you sign," Ormond said. "As you can all see, I signed the book and didn't share my crewmates' fates." Two of the creatures behind him began lumbering towards the doors. A few pirates move out of their way.

"If I get to live full of gold, why should I care about wha' happens after I'm dead," the grinning Youngen said.

And his reasoning was all it took to convince the men to start singing again and ignore the creatures that were about to attack their mates. While the pirates in front of the doors were distracted, the creature that Morrison had decapitated rose to its feet, head attached to its neck once again. The hood that covered its face had fallen off, revealing a set of black eyes sunken deep in their sockets and bloated grey skin with rips full of maggots. Fresh pirate blood dripped from its chin as it opened its mouth and jumped on Quetzal's back. Its sharp, rotten teeth sank into his neck.

Caught by surprise, Quetzal wailed in pain.

"Captain!" Doc thrust his rapier through the creature's ear.

Quetzal fell over on his side with the creature on his back. Seeing that Doc's rapier didn't stop the creature, Morrison and Reis rushed toward it and chopped off pieces of its head. When it ceased its attack, Doc kicked the body away from Quetzal's back.

Quetzal lay on the blood-soaked floor like a wounded bear. "*Curse ye*, Ormond!" One of his hands held his neck–

blood flooding through his meaty fingers–the other grabbed his chest.

"Enjoy having yer nose up the *bladdy-queen's cunt the rest of yer lifeeuug–*" A grunt of pain was the last thing that came out of his mouth.

With a sigh, Doc sheathed his rapier and lifted his hands. "I'll sign the damn book." His face showed no emotion as he retreated from the doors and the creature's path.

"You mutinous lily-livered whore!" Morrison shouted at Doc.

"My captain is dead. There is no mutiny," Doc answered without looking back or arguing against the other insults.

"And are the rest of you wharf-rat scum just going to stand there doing nothing about what you're witnessing?" Morrison asked the diminished crowd of pirates.

None of them answered or looked him in the eye.

"*Warren!*" Benson yelled.

Hearing the fear in that soft voice spread a cold feeling through Reis's chest. He wheeled in time to see the creature he'd cut in half clawing Benson's throat. Its body had reattached itself. Benson's sword stabbed the creature's face just as it had started its attack. An attack that was aimed at Reis before Benson stepped in.

Reis sprang, his cutlass swung, and he hacked the creature into pieces without realizing that the tears in his eyes were making everything blurry. He knelt and took Benson's bloodied body into his arms. The hat that kept her face hidden fell off. Her long, flaming red hair cascaded over Reis's forearm. Her lips parted as if she were about to say something, but only blood came out.

"Benson the blade was a *woman*?" Morrison asked ruefully. "All this time…" His humorless tone of voice had a hint of surprise. He snickered and stood between them and the incoming creatures.

"Her name was…" Reis's trembling hand closed her glazed green eyes. "Jodilin. The only reason I came here."

Morrison shook his head and took a deep breath, grimacing. "Hate to admit it. But I did admire you, Blaze," he exhaled slowly, "back in the good ol' days." With his sword raised, he turned and lunged toward the fiends. He lacerated and stabbed their undead-robed bodies, but they were faster than the others, and eventually, their teeth and claws found his flesh.

"*Blaze!*" Morrison yelled through blood-drenched teeth. "*Set it all on fire!*" The creatures fell on him as soon as he finished his sentence. His dissident smile never left him.

Reis had lifted Jodilin's body and was now gently placing her in a shadowed corner. His mind had drifted along the currents of the past for only a microsecond. Memories of moonlit sparring sessions that always ended in passionate embraces warmed his heart. Traces of all the times Jodilin's soft lips met his remained with him as he lamented the fact that those long-gone days had been too good, too pure to ever be allowed to last.

Once the ruminating was done, a wave of red fury washed all sentimentality away. His mind barely registered the mangled corpses on the floor, the traitors continuing to sign, or the other rats who drank their rum and pretended like nothing was happening. He reached into Quetzal's hip pocket and pulled out the dead Captain's silver flask. He opened it while simultaneously grabbing a candle from the wall.

The creatures were done gnawing on Morrison's corpse when Reis sprayed their robes and the floor in front of them with alcohol. He then ignited the liquid using the candle's flame. The creatures quickly transformed into walking infernos. The closest one swung at him. Reis darted out of the way, and its claws swished empty air before falling on top of the corpses on the floor. Its inferno found the bottles of rum and gunpowder the dead pirates had been carrying, and a line of fire burst across the floor.

Seeing the back of the cathedral in flames, the pirates in the front began to panic.

"That mad brute," the blonde Youngen coughed through the rising smoke. "We'll suffocate. Open the doors!"

"All must sign the book first," Ormond replied. The sweat from his forehead got into his eye, making it twitch.

Reis was stomping his way towards him. The second walking inferno tried to attack him but couldn't find him. The flames had melted its eyes. It ended up attacking Doc, who was the last man standing in line to sign.

"Ormond!" Doc screamed in agony while the infernal creature burned him and blindly clawed his flesh. "You said it wouldn't attack us if we signed!"

"You haven't signed yet, you imbecile," Ormond answered. The last two creatures behind him shambled forward.

As Reis got closer to the altar, they both lunged at him in spasms of ferocity. He decapitated one with a swing of his cutlass, but the other managed to stab its claws into his ribs. He kicked it back and cut off one of its legs, making it fall on top of the infernal creature that was disemboweling and scorching Doc. Finding Doc's gunpowder, the infernal creature's flames grew, drowning the three of them in the burning heat.

Reis approached the altar, not letting the pain in his ribs stop him. He pulled out his pistol and aimed at Ormond.

"You will gain nothing by killing me." Ormond's trembling hands betrayed his words. "All you had to do was sign, and you would have continued to live. But here you are. Choosing death."

"Aye! *It's a pirate's death for me.* I won't ever live like a slave down on my knees!" He changed his aim and shot the base of the silver leaver on the wall.

The lever broke and fell to the floor.

"You mad bastard! What have you done!" Ormond dropped the book on top of the altar and ran to the small opening on the wall where the lever used to be.

The coughing traitors gathering around Ormond began asking: "*Gaah*, what was that, Ormond?... What did he shoot?"

"Our only way out!" He joined their coughs while futilely trying to jam the lever back into place. "Put out that damn fire!"

The treacherous rats ran and attempted to extinguish the flames. Out of panic, the Youngens stupidly threw their ale at the inferno, igniting it further, transforming it into a fire-breathing dragon that spread burning waves through the cathedral—filling every corner with screams and smoke. Its scorching fury seared flesh, melted hair, and charred all clothing.

Blinded by fear, the few Judas left didn't comprehend the futility of trying to escape through the barred windows, and they continued to push themselves against the bars, gasping for air as the blaze cooked their backs.

The creatures were good kindling, Reis thought as he picked up the book and fed it to the flames. But the thing didn't catch fire.

"I'll see you in hell Reis!" Ormond came running and lifting his sword. Reis stopped him in his tracks by stabbing him in the heart.

"No, you won't, *rat*! You signed an agreement, *remember*? Your eternal faithful service to your parasitic whore *Queen* begins *now*." With his cutlass still in Ormond's chest, Reis dragged him backward toward the flames as if he were skewered meat. "And my name is Captain *Blaze*!" He kicked him off his blade and into the inferno.

Ormond tried to scream while he sizzled with the other burning rats and ignited creatures.

Wherever I'm going, I know I'll find her again, Reis thought, and Jodilin Benson's beautiful face flashed through his mind, warming his skin. He could almost see her fiery red hair and the shining light of her eyes as the flames engulfed him.

FIN

Looking for a horror YouTuber with the same friendly vibe of a metalhead older brother who appreciates Coppola's version of Dracula (1992) and Halloween III: Season of the Witch (1982)? *Neo-Pulps!* recommends: **Beyond the Grave Media**.

"Welcome to Beyond the Grave Media. A crypt corner specifically designed to reanimate and resurrect fright flicks often forgotten about. We'll dive headfirst into films lost in the Necropolis that deserve a rewatch and to be freed from the vault. Along the way we'll explore pulp horror memorabilia, video store titles, posters, and other frightful nostalgia. Dust off the shelves, we're breaking unhallowed ground. Cheers!" https://www.youtube.com/@BeyondTheGraveMedia. Above Artwork belongs to Beyond the Grave Media.

The Role of a Slasher

Saturday 14, February 1987

Heather Kamp ran past the many Valentine's Day decorations hanging from the hallway walls of the second floor. Now, all the cheap, red paper hearts, the cupids with their bows and arrows, and the cartoon bunnies who were supposedly falling in love were dripping blood.

The blood of Heather's friends.

With no other place to turn, she locked herself in the bathroom at the end of the hallway. The killer trailed her up the stairs. His footsteps lacerated the momentary silence that gripped Marty's lake house. It was actually his father's lake house, but Marty always bragged that he would inherit it as soon as he graduated from law school.

His yuppie dreams would never come to fruition because he was now lying naked in the master bedroom with his guts pulled out and shoved into his mouth. Stacy's decapitated head rested by his crotch, permanently gazing at him through glassy half-closed eyes. That was just one of the many gory scenes Heather had encountered tonight. The Crimson Slasher had butchered all her friends—no use questioning that fact anymore.

He's really real, Heather kept telling herself, *and I'm awake. This isn't a nightmar*e. She desperately searched the bathroom for something she could use as a weapon, not caring about all the noise she was making. She grabbed a plastic Noxzema jar out of the medicine cabinet, realized the uselessness of it, and threw it at the small window above the toilet. The glass shattered into little pieces–too small to use for stabbing or slashing. Even though she knew she wouldn't fit through the window, she stood on the toilet seat and tried anyway. All she managed to accomplish was inflict small cuts on the flesh of her neck.

"Help! For God's sake, somebody help me!" Her shrill screams echoed through the dark woods outside. She'd already done that when the Crimson Slasher chased her all around the house, and the only thing it gained her was a sore throat.

The doorknob began to rattle. The Crimson Slasher had found her. A cold wave contorted Heather's face. She felt like her heart was thundering louder than the banging on the door. The Crimson Slasher would soon break through and shove the sharp end of his butcher knife into her eighteen-year-old flesh.

How can this be happening? She stepped down from the toilet seat and pushed herself to keep looking for a weapon. She was opening the drawers beneath the sink when an unrecognizable voice from outside momentarily stopped her.

"I'm so tired of this," the voice sighed. "Can we just stop this scene for a moment... *Heather?* I know you can hear me. It's me, the so-called *Crimson Slasher*, the man who brutally ended the young lives of six of your friends. I ruined your Valentine's Day party, didn't I?"

Heather straightened up, not knowing how to answer. The fact she could hear the nonchalant tone in his voice terrified her more than the violent acts he had committed. She wanted to scream at him, threaten him, call him a *goddamn psychotic piece of shit scumbag*! But all that came out of her mouth were sobs followed by broken words: "Please, *don't*— just leave me alone. I wanna go home." The tears she'd been holding back all night came out now, fogging her view of the yellow walls that enclosed her.

"You say that as if I had a choice," the Crimson Slasher said from the other side of the door. "But I don't, *Heather!* This is the role I've been given. And I wish I could break it.

Oh, in case you're wondering how I know your name, it's because I've been stalking you guys all night, listening to all your self-absorbed, ignorant bullshit. That's right, I don't have supernatural powers. I'm a human being just like you."

"No, you're not! You're a monster!" Heather wiped away the tears with the back of her hand.

"Is that what you think?" There was a genuine tone of surprise behind his words. He didn't speak for a few seconds, prompting Heather to restart her search through the drawers beneath the sink.

"We're getting off on the wrong foot here. Let me start over," he said. "I can tell you're different. You're not drunk or high like most of my victims. I've been chasing you for almost an hour now—you should be dead already. Oh, I'm going to get you anyway, but you're sort of breaking your role. So I think you can understand what I'm trying to tell you. I wasn't born with a mask on and a knife in my hands. Just like I'm sure you weren't born screaming and crying for your life... now that I think about it, you probably were. But you can understand what I'm trying to say? Someone or something assigned us these roles, me the killer and you the victim. This wasn't our decision. Who or what is it that makes these decisions? Do they decide what we're going to be when we're born? Do they write it down on our birth certificates? Have you really looked at your birth certificate? It has a bunch of weird numbers on it, probably codes. Codes that dictate what we're supposed to be. Do you want to know what I was seven years ago before this whole stalking and murdering drunken horny teens thing started?"

Heather didn't answer. She found a nail clipper in one of the drawers, but she doubted the mini curved knife within it could do much damage, so she dropped it in the sink.

"I was an out-of-work actor," he continued, not needing a reply. "One day, this old man Moirai, hired me to scare a couple of teens who kept partying in the forest behind his farm. This rowdy bunch always left a mess. And old man Moirai was sick and tired of cleaning up after them and complaining to the cops to do something about it—which they never did. Moirai thought I was perfect for the part because of my tall build. He gave me this red, bug-exterminator, coverall jumpsuit, a butcher knife, and a *Skeletor* plastic mask that he'd spray painted red—you know from that He-man cartoon show all the kiddies seem to love so much. He told me *that* would be my mask, that it would look scary in the dark. The thing was laughable, just flimsy plastic with a string attached to it. A cheap piece of Americana, probably made in China. Little did I know how much fear that mask would strike."

Heather had been terrified by the sight of it. She couldn't believe the demonic face she'd seen hovering over the castrated corpse of Corey was just modified merchandise from a children's TV show.

"So I went there that night with the costume on," he said. "Feeling ridiculous, but enjoying the hundred bucks playing this role had gotten me. The plan was to jump out of the woods, wave the knife around, and scare those teens out of the forest forever. But there was something wrong with them. They weren't just drunk. They were high as *fuck*. When they saw me, they just sat there, staring at me, not moving from the campfire they'd built. Then suddenly, one of them pulls out a gun and starts shooting wildly, hitting his friends, the trees, everything except me. That finally made the ones who weren't shot, scream and flee in panic. One girl got up, ran, and fell on a pile of rocks, smashing her head. The shooter and what I assumed was his girlfriend jumped in their car and peeled out, driving over two of their friends in the process. I just stood there frozen, with this silly costume on and the butcher knife in my hand so clean it reflected the light of the campfire. It all happened so fast that I couldn't even process it. There were all these dead kids in front of me, and I couldn't understand how it had happened. The explosion I heard in the distance woke me up from the shock, and I got the hell out of there. A driver saw me coming out of the forest with the costume on, trying to find my truck, and that's all it took for this goddamn legend to be born," he sighed.

"The news spread fast. Exaggerated and bloated. They were calling me the *Crimson Slasher!* Never mind the fact that none of those teens had been stabbed. Hell, the last two had driven off a *goddam cliff!* That was the explosion I'd heard. But *nooo,* it was *the Slasher* who did it. Still fighting the shock and a nasty hangover, I started calling old man Moirai the next morning. He wasn't picking up the phone. I kept the knife and the costume in a bag as proof that they didn't have an ounce of blood in them. I took the bag with me when I went to see Moirai to try to explain things. I wanted him to go to the cops with me and back up my story. But what do I find when I arrive at his farm? The blasted old fool had killed himself. Left a note saying how guilty he felt for hiring a psychotic maniac. The bastard was blaming *me!*" An intimation of menace returned to his voice.

Heather realized she'd stopped searching and had been pulled into his story. She broke out of her paralysis and found a metal nail file.

"And he didn't kill himself like a real man would, shoving a shotgun on his mouth and blowing the top of his head off like Hemingway did. Or hanging himself. No. He had to do it the way 1930s Hollywood actresses used to do it. He slit his wrists in the bathtub. What kind of old man offs himself that way? And he was naked for *Christ's sake!* As I stood there in his bathroom reading over his wet suicide note, some reporters showed up. They were one step ahead of the cops. I had to escape out the back. But I couldn't take any chances, so what did I stupidly do?"

You put on the custom, Heather thought, unable to ignore his rant and acquiring a toilet plunger.

"I put on the custom to hide my identity. I flushed the suicide note down the toilet and went out the back. But of course, the reporters saw me escaping the farm. And my pictures made all the headlines, adding more fuel to the legend. A dream come true for every newscaster. *Newscasters? Spellcasters* is what they are! Those fucking vampires! You ever noticed how happy they are when reporting terrible things? And my life kept getting more terrible. It became an endless nightmare. I planned on burning the costume and throwing the knife away, even though it was just a regular butcher knife. But something kept me from doing it. I couldn't think straight, couldn't sleep. I shoved everything back in the bag and left it in the closet underneath a pile of clothes. Days passed, and made-up stories of the Crimson Slasher were all everybody could talk about everywhere I went. It made me sick. But then the worst thing of all happened. My fiancé found the costume and the knife… she freaked out, didn't even let me explain. She tried to run away from me through the fire escape of our apartment. She tripped and broke her neck on the way down," he paused.

And so did Heather. She gazed at the door, not understanding why she kept being lured back into his psychotic monologue or why he continued talking to her. *Doesn't matter why, he's giving me a chance to find a way to fight back,* she told herself. Her trembling hands unrolled the wooden stick off the rubber plunger. She put the end of the stick on the edge of the sink and started to file it with the nail file, trying to sharpen it into a stake. *This is too noisy. I better keep him talking.* "And… what did you do after that?"

It took him a few seconds to answer: "Drank like hell, thought about killing myself. Ended up driving to the police station bent on confessing to everything. Hoping they'd send me to the electric chair. On my way there my truck ran out of gas, so I stopped at a station. While I filled the tank, this van full of teens stopped at the pump across from me. They were laughing and carrying on without a care in the world. Suddenly this hatred started squeezing my head, sobering me up, turning everything red. Then I hear them talking about *the Crimson Slasher.* Saying they weren't afraid of him and that he was probably a *'fag anyway'.* The boys assured the girls that they could *'take on that pussy slasher,'* that they could '*beat the shit out of him*' if they had to! I felt like they were really talking about me! *Laughing at me!*" A deep guttural tone momentarily took over his voice as he banged on the door.

Surges of horror coursed through Heather. She couldn't hold it anymore, and the urine flowed down her leg. She avoided crying by focusing on the file, grinding the stick on one side and then the other.

"They were going to have a party at a cabin in the forest. And before I realized it, I was following them. I saw myself putting on the costume, saying out loud that this was what they wanted. That this is what some force out there wanted. It wanted me to play the role of a slasher. So I would. And I would give one hell of a performance. At midnight I burst into their cabin, and unlike the first time, they quickly reacted. Freaked out. For a moment their screams and the sight of their horrified faces pulled me out of my performance. I could see this group of scared kids looking up at an insane man wearing a cheap costume, holding a butcher knife. A man who had lost everything. Who once was young like them, full of dreams, and believed that you could decide what you wanted to be in this life. I started turning away, disgusted with myself. But suddenly, this jock kid jumped at me, and his chest found its way into my butcher knife. I couldn't believe it," he snickered.

"Two other jocks started hitting me, so I slashed at them to defend myself, and somehow, I ended up decapitating them. Complete emptiness took me over. All I felt was a blinding headache. The girls wouldn't stop screaming. I had to cut their throats to make them stop. Afterward, I went camping in a forest two towns away, waiting for the cops to come to pick me up. But they never did. All these years, I must've left fingerprints and all sorts of evidence behind, but the cops have never even questioned me. I stayed camping for a couple of months. Until this group of campers show up, shattering my peace, you can guess what happened next. I painted the forest red. I didn't question my role anymore after that. Sure, I've tried giving up many times. I moved to the desert once, and what happened? Some lost college students show up asking for directions. And my knife directed them to *hell*. I moved to an abandoned apartment building in Rainfall city. And out of nowhere, this group of troubled youths started cleaning up the place. So I *cleaned* their intestines out of their bodies. Do you see how some cosmic force out there wants me to play this role? Can you understand all of this? I'm tired of playing this role. But I don't have any other choice."

"You *do* have a choice," Heather had to speak up. "You have the choice to leave right now." She sharpened the stake as best as she could. She held it in front of her, gripping it with both hands as if it were a sword. The point of the stick wouldn't do much damage unless she aimed it at one of his eyes. *I may only get one chance.* Her heart started racing again, her body tensing up.

"I can't walk away from my role! And neither can you!" He pounded on the door, making the frame shake. "The whole universe could be thrown into chaos. And it's impossible anyway. I have tried so many times." The pounding was beginning to break the hinges.

"Just walk away, please!" Heather's legs were shaking, betraying her solid stance.

"This is a necessary role. It's the one thing I have understood." Two screws flew out of the top hinge. "I'm like cancer or alcoholism. A necessary evil meant to thin out the herd. I couldn't abandon this role unless…" The pounding stopped.

"Unless what?" Heather asked desperately. "*Unless what*?"

"Unless the role were to be recast," he finally answered after a long pause, the tone of his voice had normalized. "When Connery walked away from playing Bond, they didn't stop making those movies. They continued to make them with Roger Moore. We can recast my role. Sure. But we need to recast the victim too. So… There's only one way we could do this. Since it's just the two of us here, we'll need to trade roles."

"Wha-what do you mean?" Heather couldn't think straight anymore. Dark claws pulled at the edges of her sanity. A feeling beyond her comprehension was unfolding within her as she lowered the stake.

"Trade roles, Heather," he replied. "Someone needs to play the role of the Crimson Slasher. And somebody else needs to play the role of the victim. As the Slasher, you would get to walk away from here. My pickup truck is parked in the woods, way out back, behind a boulder. You could just keep walking straight and find it. You'll recognize the color. The keys are hidden inside an empty coffee cup by the gear stick. So what's it going to be? Do we keep playing our respective roles? Or do we tra—"

Maybe it was the exhaustion or the side effects of the thunderbolts of shock the events of this night had thrown at her, but something made her say: "*Trade!*"

The Crimson Slasher immediately broke the door open.

Heather lifted the stake, but the excessive trembling of her hands and legs diminished her strength.

The Crimson Slasher just stood in the doorway, gazing at her through the small eye holes of his red spray-painted Skeletor mask. He lifted his hand and removed his mask, revealing a shockingly nondescript face. An average American face that most people wouldn't remember. It seemed like just another mask.

Heather gazed up at him but couldn't really say what he looked like, other than that he was white and had short dark hair.

He slowly handed her the mask, and Heather took it with a trembling hand. "Put it on," he said. "The mask always goes first."

*

Heather's parents burst into her room, pulling her away from a nightmare where a guttural voice had whispered numbers into her ear.

"What is it?" Heather sat up so rapidly that she almost fell out of her bed.

"It's your friends!" Mrs. Kamp reached out and awkwardly hugged Heather's head. "Something terrible has happened!"

"Let's just take it easy now, dear." Mr. Kamp walked around the bed and sat next to Heather. The strong, woody fragrance of the Polo cologne she'd bought him for his birthday filled her whole room, waking her senses. "Heather, your friends... have been found murdered."

Heather stayed silent for several seconds, then realized she should say something. "No, what are you talking about?" She hoped her parents wouldn't hear how hard her chest was pulsating or notice how off her reaction was. She had played the role of a good, perfect daughter all her life. She played that role so well that her parents didn't even suspect she sneaked out of the house last night to attend Marty's Valentine's Day party. Or that she sneaked back in, showered the piss and blood away while watching spirals of red water going down the drain, and had fallen asleep with her hair still wet.

A white light flashed in Heather's mind, keeping her away from questioning the logic of her memories as Mr. Kamp finished telling her all the censored details of what the cops were saying had happened at the lake house.

"They believe it was the work of the… *Crimson Slasher*," Mr. Kamp said, sighing.

Those words made Heather want to throw up.

"It's a good thing I didn't let you go to that party," Mrs. Kamp said and almost wept. "I just had a feeling. A mother always knows."

Heather eyed the poorly applied Woolworth's makeup on Mrs. Kamp's face and questioned what the word mother meant. *Mother?* Heather thought, *I wonder who gave her that role?*

The phone didn't stop ringing for the next couple of days. People Heather barely knew from school or around the neighborhood offered condolences and wanted to know how she was doing and how she felt about the fact that the Crimson Slasher had killed most of her friends. But Heather knew they didn't really care about what she had to say—they didn't even wait for her to say something—so she stopped answering the phone and locked herself in her room. She spent most of the week gazing out the window or sitting on the edge of her bed, trying to figure out what had happened and waiting for something without knowing what it was.

The posters on the pink walls of her room loomed over her. Celebrities like Kevin Bacon and rock stars like Bon Jovi stared back at her through unblinking paper eyes.

All of them are acting their roles, Heather thought as she stood up, grabbed her scissors, and cut off the eyes of all the famous people in her posters, leaving pink holes in their sockets. Through a moment of clarity, she realized something was wrong with her thoughts. *What is this? Why do I keep thinking about roles?* She looked at herself in the mirror behind the door of her closet, expecting to find an answer. For the first time in her life, she studied herself as if examining a stranger. She saw she was white, athletically built, and that her long, brown, curly hair needed brushing. Other than that, she couldn't really describe what she looked like. She couldn't tell if she was pretty or not anymore. *Who decided that anyway? And why is it important?* Her face seemed like just a face. She knew some of the boys at school said she was beautiful. That's why Alan had invited her to Marty's party.

"*Alan*," Heather muttered. The last time she'd seen him, he was lying in the basement of Marty's Lake house with a pitchfork sticking out of his face. A feeling came over her that she couldn't quite understand. It was as if she had forgotten something. She tried to remember what it was and almost started screaming and crying—but then she questioned why Alan had thought she was pretty. Was it because of her popularity? And why was she popular? Did it have something to do with her being captain of the cheerleader squad, or was it because of her parents' money? That crowd of questions running through her head stomped the incomprehensible feelings that were getting in the way of her role.

"*My role?*" she questioned out loud, noticing again that something was terribly wrong. She hurried towards the living room, looking for her parents. They were sitting on the couch watching the news on TV.

Heather saw the male reporter smiling at the camera while talking about the murders at Marty's lake house. *Spellcasters!* she thought, and her mouth felt dry.

"The man the authorities have called a good Samaritan hasn't been identified," the reporter was saying. He wore large amounts of cosmetics that made his face look like a mask. "But it is believed that he was camping in the woods nearby when he heard the cries of the young victims and tried to help them before the Crimson Slasher fatally attacked him."

"Just awful," Mrs. Kamp said. "What could make someone commit such heinous acts?"

"There is no logic to people like that," Mr. Kamp replied. "They don't need a reason to do what they do. Men like the Slasher are just born evil."

"How do you know the Slasher is a man?" Heather suddenly asked, startling her parents.

Mr. Kamp quickly turned the TV off.

"Heather?" Mrs. Kamp looked at her with concern.

"What if the Slasher was a woman?" Heather questioned.

Her parents shared uneasy looks.

"Well…" Mr. Kamp rubbed the back of his neck. "That just wouldn't be possible, dear. No woman would ever be capable of doing those horrible crimes."

"That's right. We're nurturers," Mrs. Kamp stated. "Why would you think that? What's wrong?" She quickly grimaced, regretting the question.

"Mom. Dad. There's something I—" Heather began, but she couldn't stop thinking about the smile on that reporter's face.

She wanted to widen that smile… with a knife.

Heather gasped.

"What is it, dear?" Mr. Kamp stood up. "You know you can talk to us. We're here to listen."

"Listen?" Heather questioned. "We Kamps are good listeners, aren't we?" Her gaze fell to the tile floor. "A stranger could just come up to us and out of nowhere tell us about how his Fiancé died and about masks and roles, and we would just listen, wouldn't we? Was that our role? To be good listeners?" She didn't realize she was crying until she felt the tears rolling down her cheeks.

Mrs. Kamp went to her and hugged her. "I'm making an appointment with Dr. Englund tomorrow."

"I don't need a doctor." Heather slowly escaped her mother's embrace. "I just need… to see my birth certificate?"

That night, while the sounds of the neighborhood echoed through the stillness of her room, Heather stood by the open window, staring off at the street below and trying to concentrate on her thoughts. The sight of the red pickup truck kept distracting her. She had parked it across the street from her house in front of the old Miller's place that was up for sale. And no one seemed to be bothered by it or question it. Why would they? It was just the average vehicle of a handyman who was probably fixing things around the neighborhood. Who would suspect a blood-stained mask, and a jumpsuit were lying underneath the driver's seat like a terrible secret waiting to be revealed?

Mrs. Kamp knocked on the door, making Heather drop the smile that had started twitching on her lips.

"Heather, Dorothy is here to see you." Mrs. Kamp opened the door without waiting for a reply. "It would do you good to talk to someone."

Dorothy lived a couple of houses down the street. She was one year younger than Heather but always acted like she was older, richer, and more popular in school. That never bothered Heather before, but now, as she went down to see her by the foyer, the sight of Dorothy's painted face gave birth to a sudden inexplicable anger.

"Oh my God, how are you?" Dorothy's nasally voice came out through the chewing gum in her mouth. "Like, I know, *awful*. Can't even believe it." She wiped away a fake tear with a fingertip covered by a pink glued-on nail. "Wanted to say, like, I'm here for you. If you need to, like, talk. Just can't believe it. You know, I was invited to that party."

Knowing that was a lie, Heather's hands balled into tense fists. Her head ached, and she could feel the blood pulsing in her temples.

"Marty was like, all into me. Thank *God* I didn't go, *right*?" Dorothy switched the chewing gum from one side of her mouth to the other. "And thank *God* you didn't either. Can you imagine? Wanted to tell you, we're having our own wake this Friday night. At my house. I don't know if you're going to the funerals tomorrow. I haven't decided if I'll go to them all. Didn't know Tammy that well. But I'm going to Marty's and Allen's for sure. So, if there's anything you need, let me know. And drop by this Friday. The other girls are dying to–*I mean,* they want to see you. *Dying,* can you believe it? Me and my big mouth." She let out a throaty chortle, and the red gum almost came out of her mouth. "*Byii.*" She turned around and left through the door.

Heather stood there for some time, her nails digging into her palms. She stopped them only when they drew blood. She went into the kitchen and examined her mother's cutlery. She had never noticed before how sharp and beautiful the steak knife was.

The next morning, her mother questioned Heather's decision of not wanting to attend the funerals.

"It's okay that you haven't gone to school or don't want to talk to anyone." Mrs. Kamp put on a pair of golden cross earrings. "But I just don't see why you wouldn't–"

"Now, now, dear. You said you wouldn't press her on this," Mr. Kamp interjected. He took his wife by the shoulders and gently pulled her away from Heather's bedroom. "You take all the time you need," he told Heather. "Just try to eat something, or at least drink some milk. Remember that you're safe here. We'll be back this afternoon." When Heather didn't react to his words, he just smiled sadly and closed the door behind him.

Heather suddenly wanted to call out to them, tell them that she loved them. But she went back to staring out the window and questioning their roles. On the street below, the red pickup truck glistened in the sun, sending rays of light that seemed to illuminate her thoughts, making her think about how the Valentine's Day party had ended.

She finally remembered the trade she had made that night and how the deal was sealed when she'd adjusted the red mask over her face. The smell of it was nauseating, and the small eyeholes limited her vision. She'd realized what she had done when the string pulled her hair close to her head, pushing the cheap, sweaty plastic against the skin of her face.

The Slasher had unzipped his jumpsuit, taking it off, showing the white t-shirt and boxers—both had yellow and red stains—that he wore underneath.

After Heather put on the red jumpsuit that was too big for her size, the man carefully handed her the knife. Heather clutched the warm, black handle as her eyes took in the sharpness of the blade, still stained red with the blood of her friends. She couldn't believe he gave her what she needed to defend herself.

But before she could question his motives, the man lifted his hands and began to cry. "Please, I'm begging you, don't kill me," he said.

His words intensified Heather's confusion, making her mind spin. "Just move out of the way." She held the stake she'd made from a toilet plunger in one hand and gripped the knife with the other, pointing both weapons at the man.

"Whatever you say," he whimpered, slowly backing away.

Heather stepped out of the bathroom, keeping her eyes on him. She started walking backward toward the staircase.

The man immediately stopped crying. "What are you doing?"

"I'm just going home… Stay back." She threatened him with the knife.

"Without finishing your job?" A mix of anger and incredulity possessed his face. "The Crimson Slasher never leaves any *survivors*! You made a trade. Now play your role!" He started moving toward her.

Heather ran to the stairs, but he quickly grabbed her hand as she made it down the second step. Pulling her closer, he clenched her grip on the knife and forced the blade towards his chest. She pushed herself back to escape from his grasp, but he pulled her harder, dragging her down with him as he lost his balance and fell down the stairs.

With Heather on top of him, the man's back hit the floor. The landing knocked the wind out of Heather. The stake flew out of her other hand and went rolling across the blood-stained living room floor. The pain whipping down her masked forehead and neck almost made her pass out. After trying a couple of times, she successfully pushed herself away from the man and saw that the blade of the knife had disappeared into his chest. Only the black handle was visible.

The man lay still with a circle of blood forming around him. His eyes were open, staring at nothing. A slight smile seemed to be touching his red lips.

Heather couldn't understand what had happened. She squinted at the red stain expanding on the man's shirt and the knife handle protruding from his chest like an old tombstone on an unmarked grave. Gagging, she began the slow and painful process of standing up. Blurred waves scrolled down her limited vision. She was vaguely aware that Tammy's and Mike's corpses were sitting on the couch. Their throats displayed new jagged orifices.

Heather stumbled out of the lake house. Outside, the world was unbalanced and askew. Thick, black paint covered the sky, and the forest and the lake seemed to have switched places. The last thing she remembered was realizing she still wore the mask as she drove the red pickup truck toward her neighborhood.

Less than two weeks had passed since that night, but it felt like it happened years ago. And now she couldn't understand why she hadn't told anyone about it. Or why the Slasher had chosen her or why the cops couldn't figure out that the only dead adult in Marty's Lake house *was* the Crimson Slasher, not a goddamn good *Samaritan.*

Think, just concentrate and think, Heather told herself as she sat in her bed. But the only thing her mind could come up with was the fact that all her life, she had just followed the roles other people wanted her to play: The good daughter, the best friend, the sexy girlfriend, the smart student. And she could predict the roles waiting for her in the future: The good wife, the hard worker, the loving mother, the respectful citizen. *But what about the role I want to play*? she questioned. Before encountering the Slasher, she hadn't known what that role was. Although it had been there all along, hiding in the deepest corners of her unconscious mind, slithering to the surface every time she saw horror movies while pretending she didn't like them; or when she'd read about terrible crimes or one of her friends got on her nerves. *And the Slasher had known it. That's why he chose me.* She looked at herself in the mirror—like she had done more than a

64

hundred times this week—and now noticed the smile stretching her lips.

A couple of hours later, there was a knock on her door. Heather went to answer it and wasn't too surprised when she saw the cop standing in her doorway.

For a moment, she thought they finally knew she'd been at Marty's house that night, that her fingerprints were on the knife that had killed the man they were calling a *good Samaritan*. But the cop wasn't looking at her with accusing eyes.

"Miss Kamp, there's no easy way to say this," the officer began, an expression of forced sympathy dominating his tanned, clean-shaven face. "But there's been an accident… your parents…"

Heather already knew what he would say next, and she could only think about how the Slasher's Fiancé had died.

After the funeral, Mr. Kamp had drunk too much with Marty's father. Both fathers were known to be sociable drinkers. And the loss of his son probably made Marty's father demand that his friends drink with him. Mr. Kamp hadn't said no. He hadn't let Mrs. Kamp drive either. On their way home, he'd lost control of the car and smashed into an oncoming vehicle. The crash had killed him, his wife and the family in the other car. Heather hoped they had at least died instantly. The thought of how now she was an eighteen-year-old orphan crossed her mind, filling her eyes with tears that didn't roll down.

She realized the cop had stopped talking and was waiting for her to say something. "Yes, officer. I'm alright."

"Is there anyone I can call for you or—"

"Can I ask you something?" Heather interrupted him. "Did you always know you were going to be a cop?"

The officer gazed at her, confused. "What do mean—"

"You weren't born as a policeman. So, how did you know you wanted to be one? Did someone tell you that you should be a cop?"

"Well, no." The cop frowned. "Not exactly. My father was a cop. And so was my grandfather. You could say I'm just following their—"

"What about your mother and your grandmother?" Heather asked. "What were they?" The tears had disappeared from her eyes.

The cop started to answer, but then his frown deepened. "Are you sure you're alright, Miss Kamp?"

Heather nodded—bobbing her head—and tried to smile to show him how '*alright*' she was, but her mouth refused to move. It took a lot of acting on her part to convince him that she was alright. After he finally left, she closed the door and sat on the couch. Everything was clear now. She could see how the pieces had fallen into place. It was the trade she had made. She needed to accept her role.

On Friday night, carrying her mother's steak knife wrapped in a towel, she went to the red pick-up truck, opened the door, and picked up the red jumpsuit and the spray-painted Skeletor plastic mask from underneath the driver's seat.

After putting on the costume, she sneaked through the back of Dorothy's house. The wake had just been a thin excuse to hide an average teenage party. Heather waited a while, creeping around the shadows, until she found Dorothy alone in the basement.

"You decided to help after all," Dorothy said without turning around. "I mean, I'm sure Dad keeps the wine down here. Help me look… Mark?" She turned just in time to see the knife coming towards her neck. The blade cut across her jugular, opening a deep gash before she could scream.

As Dorothy's blood spattered the walls, Heather understood the necessity of her new role. And slowly, while repeatedly stabbing Dorothy's body, the teenage cheerleader named Heather Kamp disappeared and was replaced by the Crimson Slasher.

FIN

A new heavy punch of Noise Metal is about to assault listeners.

This band from Lambertville, NJ, summons elements from punk, doom, and death metal and sprinkles them with gothic melodies. If Type O Negative, Danzig, or the Misfits are constantly rotating on your playlist (and they should be if you're reading this Issue), then *Neo-Pulps!* recommends you check out **The Necrophiliac Yacht Club**. Follow their Instagram page for updates: @thenecrophiliacyachtclub

The sick above artwork belongs to/created by Kevin Harvey-drums/vocals. Jesse Somogyi-bass/vocals. Spencer Johnson-guitar/vocals.

Death is just Another Tarot Card

June 1988

The invisible hand of embarrassment slapped Arthur Wallace in the face as he told his therapist, Dr. Bellem, the details of his nightmare.

Dreams meant nothing to Arthur. But the intrusive night terror about the tarot card reader had bothered him for over a month now—waking him in the middle of most nights by squeezing his chest with the same kind of clench that nervous wrecks use to squeeze stress balls.

"It always starts the same," Arthur said, tensing up in the chair on the other side of Dr. Bellem's desk. "I'm sitting—sort of like I am now—in a black and white vintage room."

Dr. Bellem raised his grey eyebrows. "It was painted in black and white?" His German accent made the word white sound like *veit*.

"No. Everything looked black and white," Arthur clarified. "As if I was living inside an old movie. You know, like the ones with Bogart and Bacall. And I'm sort of dressed like one of those private dicks, too."

"What do you mean by private dicks?" Dr. Bellem suddenly became very interested in the details of the dream and leaned forward. His expression of overly focused attention–showing eyes that were expanding behind Coke bottle glasses–almost broke Arthur's concentration.

He always has to apply Freud's seduction theory to everything, Arthur thought, avoiding a smile. "Private detectives. Like in those classic crime movies. But the most important thing is the woman."

"Ah, so there is a woman."

"Yes. And my God, doc, she's the most beautiful woman I have ever seen. Perfect white skin contrasting against the blackness of her long dress and gloves. And even though her head is aureoled by the light coming from the fireplace behind her, her long silky hair has the color of darkness." Arthur's pulse rose with the strange mix of fear and excitement that had forced him to book this appointment.

"Go on." Dr. Bellem sucked his own dry lips to moisturize them.

"She's… she's shuffling these Tarot cards. Looks at me through dark, seductive eyes, with her crimson lips slightly parted, and for a moment, I'm enticed by her."

"You yearn for her?" Dr. Bellem asked, his words sounding more like a suggestion than a question. "You want to possess this dream woman?"

"Yes. But it's something beyond that."

"You want her, but you cannot have her."

"Something like that, but–"

"You feel like you are not man enough for her, which terrifies you."

"Yea–*wait*, no," Arthur protested. "What terrifies me is what happens next. She keeps shuffling the cards, pulls one out, and shows it to me. It's Death. She shows me the death card–the grim reaper riding a horse–and that's when it happens." He passed a hand across his forehead to wipe sweat that wasn't there.

"She suddenly throws the deck of cards on the table between us, pulls out a gun, and–*blam!* Shoots me in the chest. I feel the bullet, Doc. Feel it penetrating my chest. And that's when I wake up bathed in sweat. It's like a new kind of sick wet dream."

"What is particularly frightening to you about this dream?" Dr. Bellem asked.

"The fact that she shoots me in the damn chest! I wake up with a pain right here," he poked his own chest, right where his black tie was. "And it doesn't go away either. I can feel it right now."

"I see." Dr. Bellem tapped his desk with his gold-plated pen in a meditative way.

"And it doesn't help that I keep hearing shots all the time. I go down to get my morning coffee, and *bam*! I get out of the office–*bam*! I open a window to get some fresh air before bed–*bam*! *Bam*! I tell you, doc, my heart just can't take it anymore. They say that men as young as thirty are dropping dead from heart attacks now."

Dr. Bellem ruminated over that last sentence. His face had turned into a wrinkled mask of concern. "The city has been–as your generation likes to say– going to hell in a handbasket ever since the mayor made all those budget cuts. Crime is on the rise. Of course, you're going to hear shots."

Arthur shook his head. "You're not helping my anxiety, doc."

"However," Dr. Bellem raised his golden pen, "there is also a lot of–how do you say–*jalopies* out in the street now.

People cannot afford new cars anymore–have you seen how high those ridiculous rates have climbed?" He didn't pause to wait for an answer. "I don't even own a personal vehicle anymore. So some of those shots might just be cars backfiring."

"Maybe so, but why are they always blowing their pipes around me?" Arthur interjected.

"Ever heard of synchronicities?"

"I read all about Jung in psych 101," Arthur nodded dismissively, "and I'm not psychotic… at least not yet."

"What I mean is that coincidences happen. And it's only bad for your mental health if you dwell on them too much," Dr. Bellem said, seeming to lose interest in the conversation.

"Gun noise wouldn't even cross my mind if it wasn't for the nightmares."

"Dreams can be a way for the brain to prepare your nervous system to face life's many hurdles." Dr. Bellem's glance strayed upward to the clock on the wall. "But they're not literal. You're not going to be shot. You just became aware of how terrible the city has become. You need to get away for a little while. Man was not meant to live in this brick-and-mortar prison."

"Easier said than done," Arthur sighed. "The office has a leash around my neck and won't let go. Not for another year, anyway. Sales are down this quarter."

"What about your boss? Do the intrusive thoughts of bashing him over the head with your briefcase still possess your mind?"

Arthur tsk-tsked. "Nah, I've been doing those breathing exercises you taught me to control my anger. But those won't work to control this fear. I'm telling you, doc. There's something strange about these nightmares—"

"Do they leave you with the same unease as the ones where you were some sort of buccaneer being burned alive?"

Arthur shuddered. "Yes, but these are worse. They're even more vivid. I've always avoided all that occult mumbo jumbo stuff."

"Mumbo-jumbo?"

"Yeah, you know. Ouija boards, crystals…tarot cards."

"You do not believe in the supernatural?"

"Of course not," Arthur replied, offended.

"Tarot is just another form of divination, like the I Ching. Or flipping a coin before making a decision. Those things only have the meaning that you give them. And right now, you seem to be giving them your fear. My recommendation is for you to face these Tarot cards so you can see that they are nothing but paper and ink."

Arthur blinked heavily. "I don't see that happening anytime soon."

"That is my advice. You can take it or leave it. However, there is a chance that these nightmares will continue if you do not face your fear of the occult."

Face my fear of the occult? Jesus, he's straying far from what I've been trying to tell him, Arthur thought, feeling like a fool for wasting two hundred dollars on this session.

Dr. Bellem stood up and went over to his large bookcase. After searching for a few seconds, he pulled out a big, thick volume titled: *The Meaning of Dreams*.

"Second recommendation. Before you go to bed," he handed Arthur the book, "read about what your dreams might be trying to tell you about your mental state."

Arthur held the hardcover book in his hands. The thing was heavy, fatter than a phone book, and hard as a two-by-four. Great! Where am I supposed to carry this thing now? He opened his briefcase, shuffled some papers around, laid the dog-eared brick on top of everything, and struggled like hell to close it back up.

He was managing to secure the latches when Dr. Bellem said: "How is November for you?"

*

Arthur walked out of Dr. Bellem's office building and down Fifty-second Street, feeling two hundred dollars lighter and one useless ancient book heavier. The sun above wasn't strong enough to stab through the smog that Rainfall City was vomiting into the atmosphere. Anthills of cars were blocking the few glimpses of the horizons that could sometimes be seen through the maze of skyscrapers. Babbling noises, coming from all directions, assaulted Arthur's senses.

Doc was right, he thought, absentmindedly trying to hail a cab. *A man shouldn't live too long in this mess of cement. Is that what the nightmares are trying to tell me? To move?*

The image of the night-haired woman stirred his nerves. Made him question if what he really needed was to start dating again. An annoying little voice in the back of his mind quickly reminded him of his senior year and what had happened with Gloria, his last girlfriend. *Can't go through that again*, he told himself while another cabbie ignored him. When Gloria left him for Maximilian–the blonde, 'trust fund baby' bastard–he made a vow to himself: "When my bank account is bigger than my ego, then I'll start dating again." Right now, both things were smaller than his one-bedroom apartment.

If only things could be like they were in those Noir-Bogie-and-Bacall movies. He rented a few of them after the nightmares started, hoping to find answers. But they only left him more depressed and wishing he was one of those P.I.s, like Sam Spade or Philip Marlowe. Men like that didn't need money to get beautiful, saucy women. All they needed was a hat, a trench coat, a gun, and a whole lotta of guts.

"Guts," Arthur murmured, as the realization that he'd walked five blocks away from the business district and right into the starving mouth of lower Frankenfur made his stomach grumble. This area had turned into one of the worst parts of

Rainfall–so bad that the cops gave up on it, and supposedly, even the Crimson Slasher was using it as his personal hunting ground.

"Just what I need." Arthur spun around, and that's when he saw the Crackhead.

The man–if he could be called that–was a shaven-headed skeleton stalking towards Arthur, with hands hiding in the front pocket of a dirty, black hoodie.

This is it, Arthur thought. *It's the Grim Reaper!* He flung around and quickened his pace down the other side of the street. Most of the shops flanking the sidewalk were either closed or abandoned. *God, fucking dammit*, he griped the heavy suitcase in his hand with an urge to throw the damn thing at the Crackhead and run away like a mad bastard to safety. A car suddenly backfired in the distance, and Arthur's heart leaped so hard in his chest that his field of vision turned black for a moment. He only saw the candlelight coming from the display window of a shop. He stumbled his way to it, found a door, and went inside. The ringing of bells jarred him out of his daze. He had entered a room full of candles, crystals, incense, and various figures of deities, saints, and angels. Ice picks of fear stabbed the back of his neck.

He did it, Arthur told himself. *The Crakchead shot me, and this is what the afterlife looks like.* It took a few heartbeats for him to become aware that this was some sort of spiritual-mumbo-jumbo shop–the kind of place he had avoided all his life.

"How can I help you, young man?" The voice came from the round, gypsy-looking old lady standing behind the counter. She squinted and studied Arthur. The sleepy, tired expression on her brown, oval face disappeared. "I'm about to close, but you look like you've been seeing ghosts."

The lump in his throat prevented Arthur from uttering a cogent answer. He pivoted, gazed at the sidewalk through the display window, and let out a sigh of relief when the Crackhead kept walking, disappearing around a corner.

"Poor, little suit-bunny. Got lost in the big bad woods," the gypsy proprietor lamented. Her tone had more sympathy than mock. "Neighborhood's no good. Full of the evil juju. A good protection bracelet will take care of that. They're on sale now. *Four-ninety-nine.*"

Arthur slowly turned to face her.

"What is it, *suit-bunny*? Tell Mama Lavinia what ails ya?" Her grandmotherly smile made Arthur feel slightly safer.

And the word came out of his mouth without effort: "Tarot?"

"You want to buy a deck? Is that it?"

Arthur nodded even though he didn't want to.

"That's all?" She laughed. "I say, you poor little suit *white-bunnies* are afraid of your own shadows. Your aura says it all. Mama and Papa didn't want you messing with no hoodoo. Gave you the belt if you disobeyed, didn't they? Accused you of holding congress with the devil?"

Arthur nodded again, feeling naked.

"You reek of fear, and that says it all. My eyes have seen it all before." She gazed at him with eyes that had witnessed the less alluring aspects of life.

"Young, tall, dark, and handsome *gadjo* like you shouldn't be caring so much fear." She turned around and picked up a small red box from the shelves behind her. "City turns men into boys and boys into old men." She put the box on top of the counter and started working the register. "It's a clean five.

Gave you the nice face discount." She winked, and the beauty she must have possessed in her younger days shone through that playful expression.

Arthur had been hugging his briefcase close to his chest without giving it a thought. He let go, reached for his wallet, and pulled out a ten. "You can keep the change if you can just tell me what this is all about."

"The Tarot?"

"Everything. I don't even know how I arrived here. I just went to see my therapist because…" He told her about everything. About all the things Dr. Bellem didn't let him articulate: the nightmares, the suffocating pain in his chest, the constant creeping dread, the loneliness, the rage. And she patiently listened.

"All you have said is evidence proving what I already know. The fear is eating at you," she cooed, peering deeply into his eyes, forcing him to stare back. "You dream of being a great traveler of the seas, but are afraid of the water. You wish you were tough, but are afraid of fighting or standing up for yourself. You want a beautiful woman by your side but are terrified of them. Let it go. Say it with me."

"What?"

"Right here, right now. Say it out loud. *I let this fear go.*"

Arthur cleared his throat and tried not to feel stupid as he repeated the words: "I … let this … fear go."

"Keep repeating it daily, and you shall see how everything will change for you. Have you ever heard about the concept of past lives?"

"Like reincarnation?"

She nodded. "There are new souls–ones who are here for the first time. And old souls–ones who have been here before… Sometimes many times. You're an old soul. That is clear. You have died violently, many times."

Arthur's body stiffened. He compressed his lips so tightly that it caused him pain.

"But I do not believe your nightmares are telling you it will happen again," Mama Lavinia continued. "Maybe they're trying to warn you. The Death card in Tarot is nothing to fear. It just represents change. Transformation. Something in your old life must die before you can begin a new one. I'm willing to bet two chickens and a goat that what needs to die is that fear you're carrying in your chest."

Arthur covered his chest with his briefcase again as if shielding it. "Is this stuff for real? I mean, can it actually tell me something?"

"The Tarot will speak to you only if you are open to hearing its message." She pushed the red box towards him. "You do not need to fear them, just like you do not need to fear death. If you don't want to listen to them, then the symbols on the cards will be meaningless to you. With Death being just another tarot card in a deck full of messages you will never understand. Just like life. So give them a chance. Take it home. Sit quietly in a corner and–"

The loud banging sound of the front door closing interrupted her words.

"Why-fuc yu taking so long?" The grating voice belonged to the Crackhead Arthur had avoided earlier. Whatever junk he was on had eaten him up so much that now his skin just clung to the framework of his facial bones. He held a small, rusty old gun in his skeletal, veiny hand. The barrel aimed at Arthur.

"Oh my *Sofia*," Mama Lavinia gasped, "not again."

"Again?" Arthur exclaimed. "You said it wasn't going to happen again. This is it, isn't it? My nightmare!" He had turned completely to meet the Crackhead face to face.

"No, suit bunny," Mama Lavinia warned. "That's not what I meant…"

Arthur wasn't listening.

"Yo', throw me the wallet *Matha'fucka*. And-and tha' suitcase *too*. Yu' made me wait enough." The Crackhead looked over Arthur's shoulder. "Ol' bitch! Get with tha' rhy'em. Empty tha' register."

"I'm only thirty years old," Arthur said and then screamed it. "I'm only thirty years old! This isn't fair!" A fit of unfamiliar anger rose inside him, pushing his legs towards the Crackhead.

The Crackhead's beady eyes twitched. "Wa'chu doing fool?"

"A beautiful woman was supposed to shoot me. Not you! I can't even get a hot woman to shoot me. Why is that, huh? Why can't nothing ever go my way?"

"This fool crazy!" The Crackhead squeezed the trigger. The noise reverberated all through the shop as the bullet punctured Arthur's briefcase moments before he lifted it and brought it down on the Crackhead's face.

The Crackhead gurgled what sounded like a shout of pain. He fell backward, banging out another bullet that flew too close to Arthur's ear. Arthur dropped to his knees on top of him and repeatedly smashed him in the face with the corners of the briefcase. By the time the Crackhead had loosed his grip on the gun, the few teeth he'd had left were now sticking to a corner of the briefcase, glued to it thanks to a mix of his blood and saliva.

*

Arthur squinted as the red and blue lights of the cop car kept flashing in his face. Something had been unlocked inside of him, a weight lifted. Nothing bothered him. The stuffy heat of the summer night, the used syringes and trash littering the sidewalk where he was sitting, the constant banshee wailing of the city, and the hole in his nine-hundred-dollar suitcase that was big enough to fit his pinky finger were all just trivial things now. Drifting whimpers in the back of his mind.

"You're lucky it was only an old twenty-two caliber," the police officer told him. He was a large, African American mustachioed man, not doing a very good job of hiding a smirk while writing down in a pocketbook. "We're going to have to keep that book as evidence. Bullet's still stuck in it. What are you anyway? Some sort of head doctor?"

"No, officer." Arthur gazed up at him. "I just work in sales."

"If you go around smashing every junkie that comes at you, you won't be doing any more selling. The next one might be packing an Uzi. No briefcase can stop that." The officer closed his pocketbook, seeming to be satisfied with all the facts, and walked away. The Crackhead was still unconscious in the back of the patrol car, his face a mushy mess of blood and snot.

"Suit bunny!" Mama Lavinia called from the doorway of her shop.

Arthur stood up, walked over to her, and his heart suddenly stopped for a second.

The woman from his nightmare was emerging from the darkness inside the shop. She stood next to Mama Lavinia and smiled.

Arthur couldn't believe it. A few small details were different, like her hippie clothes and the lack of makeup, but everything else was the same. She looked more earthy now, yet her fine features still held that aura of old-world glamor that had made the world of his nightmares seem like a black-and-white film.

"I want you to meet my daughter," Mama Lavinia said proudly. "Mia, this is the bunny that–"

Mia took a step forward and put her arms around him, hugging him tightly. A quiver of ecstasy cascaded through Arthur's body as her rounded, petite breasts pressed his chest, right where the pain had been.

"Thank you for saving my mother," she whispered into his ear, almost making him lose consciousness.

"Third time that bastard tried robbing me," Mama Lavinia was saying, but to Arthur, her words were echoes coming from a faraway land. "Threatened to kill me the next time if I didn't have enough money…"

Mia released him, stepping back. He almost prevented her from doing it. Dumbfounded, he couldn't tear his gaze away from her, from every detail of her frame. His eyes devoured her slender curves, her tan skin, and the facial features that seemed to come straight out of a Pulp Magazine.

She hesitated, struggling to say something over the words that continued to come out of her mother. She smiled but then noticed how Arthur was gazing at her. She mirrored his stare, and unbelievably, a tiny hint of seduction possessed her eyes. The hint grew more robust, and the impossibility of this situation suddenly dawned on Arthur. Nervousness made him drop his gaze towards her mouth. That didn't help because now he wanted to taste the nectar of her parted lips.

"Mama," she told her mother without removing her gaze from Arthur's face. "I think that cop wants to talk to you." Her hand gave Mama Lavinia's back a slight push towards the direction of the patrol car. Her mother seemed to get the hint and paused her long diatribe against Rainfall's judicial system.

"Oh, yes…there's a few things I must spell out to those Coppers." Mama Lavinia sauntered away.

"Have we met before?" Mia asked Arthur, wrinkling her brow. "I have the strangest feeling that I've seen you somewhere, maybe?"

You've been seducing and shooting me in the chest almost every night, Arthur thought and absentmindedly said: "If Cupid were real–here in modern times–he would be using a gun instead of a bow and arrows, wouldn't he?"

She snorted. "What?"

"Uh, never mind–"

A demonic entity raised the volume of the city, and their attempts at conversation were abruptly cut by the screeching and howling of the night.

"This place gets worse every year," Mia lamented. "We shouldn't be standing here. As soon as the cops leave, we should take off."

Arthur panicked. "No–I mean, is there any way I can meet you somewhere? For a cup of coffee?"

"I don't drink coffee. It's as bad as the crack that's turning all these people into zombies." She flashed him a smile. "But I drink tea. I know this great tea house on 4th Street. But they're close now."

"What about tomorrow?" Arthur hoped she wouldn't hear how hard his heart was beating.

A shadow of sadness crossed Mia's gorgeous face. "I have to catch a flight in the morning."

"What?" Arthur's heart dropped, and the negative thoughts came back. *I don't get it. What does any of this mean, then? What should I do? What do I say without sounding like a creep?*

"I'm returning to Chikchan. It's a small, snake-like island in the Caribbean. I can't stand this city. Been trying to convince Mama to leave, but she's so stubborn."

"Chikchan?" Arthur questioned, with the inquisitive air of a city dweller who has never traveled more than twenty miles away from homebase.

Mia nodded. "It's paradise. And of course, like any paradise these days, it's been attracting Corporate Leeches. Me and my friends have been protesting their deforestation by day and living rent-free by the beach at night. We're sort of like a throwback commune. Like a modern back-to-the-land movement." There was a slight drop in her confidence as she said: "I know this is totally wild, but there's something about you… You–you're welcome to come. If you're interested in leaving this hell behind." The hope in her eyes stripped away all the annoying thoughts that were resurfacing in Arthur's mind. Those weak little voices that had held him back all his life, that had fed him constant worst-case scenarios and had prevented him from enjoying his adulthood. Arthur started nodding without realizing it, too busy knowing that this woman had really shot him in the chest and had killed his old life. She was the beginning of what he had always wanted, and no fear could stop him from enjoying it. His memory flashed a quote from a Humphrey Bogart movie: *I was born when I met her and lived while she loved me, but now I'll die if we grow apart.* He invoked that hardboiled Bogartian spirit, stared deeply into Mia's eyes, and said: "Can we have that cup of tea by the beach then?"

Her bright, shining smile was the only answer he needed.

FIN

If you've been craving to read a Pulpy horror novel that mixes elements of dark fantasy, syncretism, conspiracy theories, and occult knowledge, then *Neo-Pulps!* recommends you stay tuned for the upcoming 1st episode of the Melindra Macia series ***Melindra and The Damned*** by Melanie Ramos: June 2000. Eighteen-year-old goth girl Melindra Macia lives a boring but quiet life in the town of Henenlotter. One day, three men show up, claiming to be a vampire, a werewolf, and a zombie. And they tell her that she's a True Healer—someone with the power to heal wounds, diseases, and curses. This revelation pushes Melindra into a dark world of monsters, demons, superpowers, cults, and conspiracies where she'll have to protect her life and her own mental sanity. Instagram: @melindraandthedamned.

The Serpent in The Forest

September 23, 1989

"When I told Gordon to send me the best snake hunter he could find," Ferderlanc told Chiagon while she climbed onto the back of the jeep, "you weren't exactly what I was expecting."

She'd noticed that he was discreetly studying her tall, almost muscular body and outfit: a camouflage jacket with rolled-up sleeves, brown cargo pants, and black boots that had seen many years of use. His bloodshot eyes had avoided staring at the scar that slid across her right forearm by briefly scanning her tanned face and the long black hair she'd strangled into a ponytail.

"Don't get me wrong, I'm all up for women's lib and what-not, but I didn't know there were any China-women hunters," he explained from the front passenger seat, letting out a nervous chuckle as the driver pulled out of the airport's parking lot, heading into a short highway.

I'm half-Japanese, you walking-heart-attack, Chiagon thought, already grinding her teeth. *And you're exactly what I'd imagined when Gordon told me a wealthy American land developer had hired me.*

Ferderlanc was a small, overweight, middle-aged, sun-burned white man drowning in sweat. The brown Hawaiian shirt sticking to his flesh did a poor job of soaking it all. An expensive Panama hat covered his probably balding head. He kept a meaty hand on it to prevent the wind from blowing it away.

"It takes all kinds, I suppose…" He shrugged. "As long as you can take care of those goddam' things trying to stop our progress." He turned around to face her. "You can exterminate them all, can you?" He arched his bushy gray eyebrows.

Chiagon nodded slowly, expressionless, and looked directly into his eyes for the first time. Her mind flashed an image of her hunting knife plunging into the skull of a viper.

Ferderlanc turned away, satisfied and confused by the hatred in her eyes. "Don't get me wrong. I'm not frightened by them like these superstitious natives. Hell, I saw all kinds of snakes in Vietnam. They killed as many soldiers as *the goddam'* Vietcong."

The greenery on the right side of the highway showed glimpses of the ocean beyond, and the water sometimes reflected spears of morning light through branches and leaves. Chiagon wanted to fully see what the beach looked like, but the trees and bushes kept blocking her view.

"Some of my boys started catching them and drinking their blood," Ferderlanc droned on. "They thought snake blood would give them superpowers or something. I let them do it. Whatever got them to defeat the enemy was alright by me… Still don't know how they managed to lose that war. Too much whining from back home killed their spirit, I suppose. Man's gotta keep up his *spirit*! Ain't that right, Enrique!" He slapped the driver on the shoulder.

The driver, a timid, haggard-looking Hispanic old man, almost lost control of the jeep. "Is a good Captain," he said with a heavy accent, nodding and grinning as if nothing had happened.

"For Christ's sake, ya idiot!" Ferderlanc held on to the dashboard. "Watch the road, *will ya*!" The veins on his neck bulged like the body of a python who just fed.

An almost painful irony had been haunting Chiagon since Gordon, a representative of The Fish and Wildlife Conservation Commission, had told her that Ferderlanc used to be an Army Captain who had served in Vietnam. But was that really what was haunting her and robbing her of sleep? Or was it the person she used to be?

In what felt like a lifetime ago, she'd been a young, idealistic girl protesting that war. Supported by the flower power movement of the 60s, she had fought against the Ferderlancs of the world, had promised to protect all living creatures, and had lived day by day with love always in her heart. And here she was now, twenty years later, working for what had once been her enemy, destroying rather than protecting and being controlled by hatred like puppet strings pulling her from job to job.

I can't be haunted by a person who never existed, she told herself, unconsciously touching her scar. The highway had been replaced by a barely paved road with wooden houses and dilapidated shacks crowding in on both sides.

"… once all of this is replaced by the best hotels and restaurants of the mainland, they'll say it was the great Captain Ferderlanc who brought the 80s into the island of Chikchan…" Ferderlanc continued to spew an endless stream of words.

Chiagon was only half-listening while watching the natives as they passed them by. She mostly saw barefooted children running and playing across narrow dirt roads and a few old men sitting on the boarded floors of their balconies. She'd read in an article that a decade ago, many of the healthy women of this island had left their homes to go find work in the States. Some of them did find employment and managed to send money to their families when they could, but most were never heard from again. This left many children on the island on their own since, during the day, a lot of the fathers had to work in whatever jobs they could find. Construction and deforestation were the biggest sources of employment now. And Ferderlanc was the king of both sectors. He was paying these natives to destroy their own habitats, and decades of living in poverty blinded them to the consequences of what they were doing.

"Look at these filthy kids, running around wild like monkeys," he snarled in disgust. "District can't afford to build any more schools to lock them up. Their selfish mothers ran off, and now they got their fathers dropping dead from goddam' snake bites of all things—I tell you, they should build me a statue for all the good I'm doing for them."

The jeep slowed down as a group of teens carrying buckets and homemade fishing rods crossed the road. A much younger, dark-haired, shirtless boy tailed along. He was playing with a brown belt, choking it with one hand as if it were a cobra. Chiagon wondered how old he was.

Probably around four, she thought. *Same age as Moon was when—now why the fuck would you think about that*! She put a hand on her forehead, pretending to massage it but wanting to bury her fingernails into her flesh.

Despite the hot weather, she suddenly felt cold. Nothing about this job was right. Taking it had brought back a past that was now screaming to be heard in the back of her mind.

"...It was bad enough going against the Historic Preservation committee after word got out that we were digging into some ancient ruins or some such *nonsense*. All that fuss over some *stone-church* where the British used to pussy-foot around. If you ask me, what the committee was really after was pirate *gold*. Oh yeah, you may laugh. But pirates used to roam around all these parts. Using this very ground as a hiding spot for their loot..."

A never-ending stream of blabber poured out of Ferderlanc's mouth while Chiagon's mind reeled. He finally showed her the land where his workers had been attacked and explained how the rest of the workforce kept threatening to quit if something wasn't done about the snakes.

A few meters away, Chiagon spotted a group of protesters—who didn't seem to be natives—converging on an unpaved road across the site.

"Goddam hippies!" Ferderlanc snarled. "See what I mean? They never went away. Traitors always getting in the way of progress." He stuck his head out the window and barked at the protestors like a mentally challenged dog: "*Bahr, bahr!* Get the hell off my property! And take a damn shower! *Shuee!*"

To Chiagon, the mostly white youngsters in the group resembled flamboyant gypsies more than hippies. "I need to look around," she suddenly blurted, surprising herself and Ferderlanc.

"Well, sure," Ferderlanc replied, "but be careful of those rat-bastards. And I haven't shown you where you'll be staying—"

Chiagon stepped out of the Jeep and quickly walked into the forest that was slowly being transformed into the base of a future resort. The noises of machinery, axes stabbing the flesh of trees, and the protesting echoes coming from the colorful cluster of well-meaning youths had replaced all the calming sounds of nature.

Chiagon had hoped getting some fresh air would block the past from slithering into her present, but the exhaust fumes and the sounds of activism just intensified the suffocation that had attacked her in the Jeep. She pretended to examine the perimeter and then forced herself to return to the Jeep. She told an annoyed Ferderlanc that she would take care of the problem tonight. Snakes were mostly nocturnal creatures, and so was she.

They dropped her off at a run-down bungalow that was masquerading as a motel while Ferderlanc went across the street to the five-star Hotel where he was staying. That white, twenty-three-floor, brick-Leviathan was the first of its kind on this island. And it loomed over the whole village. Drowning everything in its shadow.

The shadow of 'progress,' Chiagon thought as she went into her room. *Didn't you used to attend lectures against this kind of 'progress,'* a voice in her head said. *You know what happens next, don't you? The gentrification, the relocations, and more trees being chopped down so they can build their parking lots, golf courses, and fast-food chains—* "Shut up!" Chiagon said out loud.

She lay back in the small bed and gazed at the ophidian-shaped cracks in the ceiling. "Why are you torturing me now?" she asked the voice in her head. But only the silence of the room answered her. "What do you want me to do? I'm not on a hero's journey. I'm nobody's hero."

She realized she was talking to herself in an empty room and told herself that these were the side effects of not sleeping for almost three days in a row. She closed her eyes. A few seconds later, a shape began to uncoil in the darkness behind her lids, forcing her to open her eyes again as the voice came back: *All you have to do is remember*.

She had once been known as Asami Kennelly, a loving wife and mother. She'd left her activism days behind when her son Moon was born. She went to raise him with her husband, Douglas, in a blissfully happy commune in South Florida. All went well until the day the Kukulkan rattlesnake came.

It happened on a beautiful June afternoon. Moon was playing in the forest when his tiny leg was bitten. They tried to take him to the hospital as fast as they could. Asami sat with him in the back of the car as Douglas drove at high speed. Moon kept repeating the word *chiagon*, and through the fog of fear in her mind, she realized he was trying to say *Chinese dragon.* She used to read to him stories from a book about Chinese mythology.

"What's he saying?" Douglas had asked in desperation.

"*Chiagon*, Chinese dragon. He must've thought what bit him was a Chinese dragon," she'd whispered through her tears.

"What was he saying, Asami?" he had turned around to look at them, and as Asami answered "*Chiagon*" one more time, he lost control of the wheel, and the car smashed into a tree on the side of the road. The accident killed Douglas, but the coroner said that Moon had already died before the crash. Asami had been thrown shoulder-first through the windshield, landing on some bushes several feet away into the wetland. They told her she was lucky to be alive when she woke up from a two-week coma.

But she knew the truth.

That day, Asami Kennelly died, and Chiagon had been born. Soon after that, the commune where she had lived disbanded. The land was sold to a corporation that quickly turned it into a resort. But not before they hired a snake hunter to exterminate the rattlesnake problem. This was how she discovered that one could make a living hunting snakes. So she spent years studying Ophiology, then learned how to capture and kill them, eventually becoming the best hunter in the States.

And now here she was, twenty years later, and the pain was still haunting her. Tormenting her as the sky outside crawled into darkness and slender shadows streaked in through the window. The past tightened its grip on her consciousness while she gathered her gear and pushed herself to do her job.

Enrique the driver was supposed to take her to the site, but she decided to go on foot, alone. By the time she arrived at the forest, the voice had returned. She ignored it and used a small flashlight to illuminate the low foliage, planning to take out as many snakes with her hunting knife as she could find. After that, she would set up some minnow traps that she would check back tomorrow night. But what she discovered hiding behind a log destroyed her whole plan.

It was a Kukulkan rattlesnake.

The same kind that had killed her son all those years ago.

The Kukulkan started shaking the rattle on the tip of its tail. Its slit-like elliptical pupils turned towards her. Its reddish-green body coiled tightly, readying itself for an attack before she had time to process all of this. Bending, she automatically pulled out her sharp hunting knife from its sheath and sliced off the Kukulkan's head as it was baring its fangs.

It was an amateur way to kill a snake since the decapitated head could still bite. So she quickly stepped back, away from the head. And now she could hear more rattling all around her.

They're everywhere! she thought as the loud buzzing sound intensified. Blood pounded agonizingly in her temples. *This can't be happening. The Kukulkans are a rare species mostly found in swamp areas, not in this type of forest— unless…* A revelation slithered into her mind as she listened to the rattling rhythm that seemed to be speaking to her. And beneath the glow of the moonlight, she understood what the real problem was and finally listened to the voice in her mind.

. .

It was easy to find Ferderlanc's room on the third floor.

Chiagon climbed through the balcony and found him passed out on his bed with an empty bottle of tequila at his side.

She woke him up with a few slaps to the face. Confused and squinting at the light of

her flashlight, he immediately started protesting. "Wha', are you crazy? You can't just barge into my room like—"

"They got out of control, didn't they?" she asked him, picking up two bags and shaking them, making them rattle. "Were you using them to kill a few natives so you could take their land?"

"What are you talking about? What do you have in those bags?" He widened his eyes.

Chiagon let him see by throwing the rattlesnakes on his bed, making him scream. "These are rare Kukulkan rattlesnakes. They're not from this island. You brought them here, didn't you? So they could do your dirty work? So you could build more resorts, just like you did in South Florida?"

"You're insane. I haven't built anything in Florida! And there's no such thing as *Kukulkans!* These are just native rattlesnakes! What's wrong with *ya*? Help—" He tried to get up from the bed, but two of the snakes lunged at him. One bit his forearm, and the other sank its fangs into the bulging vein in his neck. He fell over the bedside table, making the other snakes attack him. His screams turned into chokes. His hands tried to pull the snakes away, then gave up as he rolled over and dropped on the floor, clutching at his chest.

Underneath the loud vibrating of tails, Chiagon could hear Enrique the driver knocking on Ferderlanc's door while she escaped down the balcony, not leaving any evidence behind.

The rattling voice disappeared as she walked through the village's gloom-infested, desolated dirt roads, hoping to find all those motherless children who needed her protection; and feeling like she had shed her skin now that she'd finally killed the real serpent in the forest.

FIN

If you've been looking for an excellent werewolf-stoner, black comedy to read on Halloween, *Neo-Pulps!* recommends **Moon High: A Werewolf drug comedy** by Maxwell Shepherd:

In the small California town of Wood, mysterious beast creatures stalk the night. One of them is Eric, a lonely stoner and werewolf. With the help of his new best pal, Eric must put a stop to a spate of recent murders while also seeking to control his werewolfian impulses in this gore-soaked buddy comedy. Available digitally through most eBook platforms. Paperback available on Amazon. To keep up with his current projects or just enjoy some hilarious posts, follow Maxwell on Instagram at @maxwheelsheephard.

With a Little Help from the Rain

October 2054

The rain hissing in the darkness of the empty streets muffled the thumping sounds of his own beating heart. He plodded forward with his head slightly bent down, trying to avoid being drenched and not wanting to acknowledge the skyscrapers above him. Those intimidating concrete giants that made him feel small and meaningless in this cold city. He needed to escape their towering omnipresence.

The flying silver saucers tricked him into raising his gaze. They went swooshing through the sky–methodically avoiding the H-towers as they penetrated the penumbra of the

alleyways with their navigation beacon lights–searching for
vermin to disintegrate.

"Pest control," he murmured. His consciousness hinted
at the proper name for the saucers, a word that sounded like
Drown. "Yes, I am drowning." He wiped a mix of perspiration
and raindrops from the back of his neck.

When the rain finally ceased, he realized he must have
been trudging through this black abyss of vacant sidewalks for
almost two hours now without seeing a single soul.

Maybe this is a blessing, he told himself. *Don't need
any suspicious eyes calling the cops. But I need to find a
payphone before they find me*. An image of their bright lights
intensifying the whiteness of their walls flashed through his
mind. *No! They won't take me back there again*. He had to
remind himself to breathe as he quickened his shuffling gait.
*Gotta call old Sarge. He's the only one who can help me. But
where are the payphones? Where is anything in this damn
city?* The street signs around him were like the hostile faces of
strangers in a crowd. *They can't keep me trapped in here!* he
almost shouted before he heard a car approaching.

His heart started drumming again. *Please don't be a cop*, he threw a backward glance, ready to take off running. A black limousine was slowly slithering in his direction as if it were an alligator hunting for prey. He calmed down, but kept walking, knowing that no rich bastard was ever going to help him. He was very surprised to hear a window rolling down as the limousine stopped beside him.

"I say there, young fellow, you must be very brave?" A white old man asked through the window. "Don't you know about the virus?"

"What?" he paused mid-stride. For a second, he thought the old man was making fun of him, setting up some one-percenter joke that he couldn't understand.

"Haven't you heard of it?" The blue eyes on his aristocratic creased face seemed to study him like a zoologist fascinated by an endangered species. His white mustache and hair were perfectly trimmed, accentuating his professorial image. "You're not supposed to be out walking about."

"I-I was, just looking for a pay phone," he replied.

"*Payphones*? There aren't any payphones in Rainfall anymore," Old-blue-eyes scoffed. There was laughter behind

113

him. "Last one was taken down probably when you were a child. What is your name?"

My name? he thought, and the instant panic of being unable to answer such an easy question drowned him in the coldness of the night. After his lungs pulled in much-needed air, he gasped the name of one of the streets he'd passed by: "Doyerson."

That produced more laughter from inside the limousine, but Old-blue-eyes didn't react to it. "If you need to communicate with someone, *Mr. Doyerson*, I can offer you the use of my Adrenophone."

The limousine's door opened, inviting Doyerson in before he could think of what to say. He hesitated, assessing the situation. Around him, the streets remained devoid of life, and their shadows were ready to swallow him up as soon as he let his guard down. The light that came from inside the limousine seemed to be his only choice.

Slowly stepping inside, he became aware of the two other old men. One was big, bald, and wore gold-rimmed glasses that magnified his black eyes–which barely showed any white. He was sitting next to Old-blue-eyes with a smile stretched across his white face. An older, silver-haired Asian man sat across from them. His tiny grey eyes, planted deep in wrinkled flesh, revealed nothing, just like his face. He slid away from Doyerson, either out of aversion or to give him room.

Doyerson couldn't tell which. He sat down beside the Asian man, feeling self-conscious about his wet pajamas. The men around him wore somber, tailored suits made from cashmere fabrics that displayed a patina of extreme wealth. Their golden jewelry stood out like stars in a black sky. Doyerson had automatically closed the door and regretted it as soon as he did. The overpowering smell of alcohol and the low temperature inside the limousine increased his dizziness. The black and white checkered carpet around him didn't help either.

This was a mistake, he started to move towards the door.

"You must tell me," Old-blue-eyes gestured with his Adrenophone in his hand, "what gave you the strength to walk away from the hospital?" His eyes studied the plastic medical wristband around Doyerson's left wrist.

"Hospital?" Doyerson whispered, and all at once, the images came: bright lights, yellow floors, bodies on gurneys, veins on necks bulging. He trembled as his blurry vision registered the Adrenophone Old-blue-eyes was trying to give him. "I can't call Old Sarge," he thought out loud, a sudden pain gripping his bowels. Old Sarge, a veteran of two wars, the strongest man he had ever known, had been struck down by an invisible enemy. He had died in his cabin in the woods some time ago, coughing and suffocating, like all those people back in the hospital.

"*They won't get me in one of them hospitals*," he'd said the last time Doyerson had gone over to see him. "*When I draw my last breath, it will be in this fresh air, among the trees.*"

Doyerson couldn't remember Old Sarge's name. But the image of the solitary crow he'd spotted stalking around the grass in Sarge's front yard refused to leave him. Just one lone-wolf crow searching for food, finding none, and flying off into the bleak sky that was peppered with more saucers than stars. Doyerson had noted it as an omen then, while agreeing with Sarge's last statement.

A statement that his fear would make him go against when the invisible enemy paid him a visit in the middle of the night. He ended up going to the city's hospital, looking for help. After hours of seeing all those strangers around him drawing their last breath out of the disinfected air, under those bright lights that illuminated every twitch their bodies made as the disease ate their lives away, he couldn't take it anymore, and he had to escape. He ran away from the hospital as most of his memories started to leave him.

"Well, didn't you need to call someone? Or is everyone you know dead?" the big old man asked him and laughed.

"What's—what's happening?" Doyerson mind clouded again.

"You're in stage one, young fellow. The confusion, with memory lapses. A brilliant beginning in the good Doctor's fantastic design. Spread all around with a little help from the rain," Old-blue-eyes smiled with pride. "Soon, the coughing and the throat constriction will begin. But before that, you must tell me how you are finding the strength to fight it?" His blue eyes widened.

"To fight what?"

"Well, the virus of course. What made you walk all this way? It couldn't just be the need to make a call. What is it that you're really looking for?"

"I don't know anything about a virus." Doyerson buried his face in his hands and spoke about the only things that were in his mind, even if they didn't make any sense to him: "It's not natural. To go under those bright lights inside the belly of one of those giants. Death is supposed to happen in the darkness. Under a real sky, with real air. Not in this concrete hell!"

"There it is!" The big old man laughed, pointing a thick finger toward Doyerson. "Your indomitable human spirit! Hick-boy just wants to get out of the city, wants to die in the country. Nothing to do with being brave. How pathetic. Collected enough data yet?" he asked Old-blue-eyes.

"Yes. Very disappointing," old-blue-eyes replied thoughtfully, returning his Adrenophone back to his pocket.

"We wasted enough of our time," the Asian old man grunted in disgust, his arms folding across his chest.

Doyerson heard the door being opened. He removed his face from his hands and realized he had been crying. "Who are you people?"

Old-blue-eyes studied him for a few seconds. "We are mere spectators in a grand design... Architects in a great reset," he gestured towards the open door. "Now, if you'll be so kind, we've given you enough of our time."

Doyerson stepped out, struggling with his balance. By the time he had managed to turn around, the limousine was already gone.

And so was his memory of them.

He stood on the sidewalk for a while, coughing, until he remembered he had to keep moving—that he needed to get away before those bright lights found him. So he started trudging once again, eventually merging with the many shadows haunting Rainfall City.

FIN

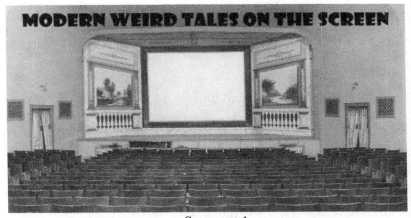

MODERN WEIRD TALES ON THE SCREEN

Segment 1

In May of 2024, the king of Indie Pulp films, Roger William Corman, passed away. His death marked an end to an era where weird tales used to reign supreme in Television screens, Drive-ins, Grind houses, and Video stores. Sure, we still have people like Uncle Joe Bob keeping the spirit of that era alive. But what about filmmakers? If the name B. Harrison Smith doesn't sound familiar to you, then maybe the titles of some of his best Pulpy films will:

The Fields (2011), scripted by Smith, is a dark and disturbing piece of neo-southern gothic cinema. With a plot that makes excellent use of the panic the Manson murders injected into people, showing hints of the "hippie phobia" that began in 1969. Smith's script used this concept of "transient-hippie-paranoia" before Tarantino peppered "Once Upon a Time in Hollywood" with it.

Camp Dread (2014) did something different with the Slasher genre, mixing gory scenes that sometimes catch you in the eye (wink, wink) with an interesting plot that makes you question what the real purpose of those *MTV* reality shows from the 90s like *The Real World* was. To psychologically torture their contestants? If you ask one of the main characters, unhinged writer/director Julian Barrett (played by Erick Roberts—who also played a similar character in 2006's campy Dead or Alive), he probably would say yes. The film also stars the amazing Felissa Rose, known to the Mutant family as Aunt Rose (AKA: Mangled Dick Expert).

Death House (2017) was a fun party flick so full of horror legends that you won't stop geeking out about it.

And the main subject of this segment:

The Special (2020). Saying that the plot of this movie is weird is an understatement. I can see screenwriters James Newman and Mark Steensland invading Mr. Smith's office and telling him: "We have this script here… it's about a box… Do you have the guts to direct it?" Then Mr. Smith getting up from his chair, taking a shot of whisky, looking at the screenwriters straight in the eyes, and answering: "Fuck yeah, I do. Gentlemen, let's shoot this fucker!" (He probably doesn't drink or curses that much–but that's just our Pulpy way of imagining everything. *Please don't cancel us, Mr. Smith*).

The Special is such a bizarre, original concept that Farnsworth Wright would have immediately published it in one of Weird Tales Issues—he probably would have edited all the sex stuff, though. The heavy theme of addiction runs rampant through this one, as Jerry (Davy Raphaely, who also shows up in Camp Dread) seeks revenge against his wife's supposed infidelity. His friend, Mike (played by the hilarious Dave Sheridan, from Scary Movie fame), takes him to a brothel where he is introduced to *the Special*. Giving away anything more than that would be a disservice, but just know, the horror comes from making you realize what the life of a sex addict, junky, or an alcoholic must be like. And it does it all through the use of weird fiction.

B. Harrison Smith is an independent creator with a long career worth checking out. This little resume only scratched the surface, but it's enough evidence to prove that there are still directors out there keeping the Corman spirit alive. For more information about his work, check out his website at www.class85.com or his Instagram @smithbharrison.

We are not paid advertisers, just Pulp fans.

Thank you for making it this far and follow us for updates: Instagram/@neopulps

YouTube/@Neo-Pulps

Website/neopulps.com